When the Road is Narrow

WHEN THE ROAD IS NARROW

An Introduction to Christian Discipleship

Kyle Nance

Narrow Valley

©2023 by Narrow Valley, LLC
All rights reserved.

Published in the United States by Narrow Valley, LLC, Mount Juliet, TN

No portion of this book may be reproduced in any form without written permission from the publisher or author, except as permitted by U.S. copyright law.

Scripture taken from the Holy Bible, New International Version®. NIV®. Copyright © 1973, 1978, 1984 by International Bible Society. Used by permission of Zondervan. All rights reserved.

When denoted with "NKJV," Scripture taken from the New King James Version®. Copyright © 1982 by Thomas Nelson. Used by permission. All rights reserved.

This publication is designed to provide accurate information in regard to the subject matter covered. Neither the author nor the publisher is engaged in rendering legal, investment, accounting or other professional services. While the publisher and author have used their best efforts in preparing this book, they make no representations or warranties with respect to the accuracy or completeness of its contents. No warranty may be created or extended by sales representatives or written sales materials. You should consult with a professional when appropriate. Neither the publisher nor the author shall be liable for any loss of profit or any other commercial damages, including but not limited to special, incidental, consequential, personal, or other damages.

ISBN 979-8-9891196-0-8

Table of Contents

Introduction		1
Part One	Milk	
Chapter 1	Disciplines of the Faith	7
Chapter 2	Faith Saves	33
Chapter 3	You Are Forgiven	49
Chapter 4	The Omnis of God	61
Part Two	Cheetos and Cheerios	
Chapter 5	Jesus, the Lion	85
Chapter 6	Choosing Your Friends	101
Chapter 7	Judge Yourself	115
Chapter 8	Master the Tongue	131
Part Three	Meat	
Chapter 9	How to Read the Bible	141
Chapter 10	Be Content	157
Chapter 11	As in the Days of Noah	181
Epilogue		203
Acknowledgements		207
Bibliography		209
Scripture Index		213

Introduction

There is an epidemic sweeping the nation; the world, in fact. Indeed, our world, our nation—our state, county, and city are all infected. It has permeated those places that are most sacred to us. Our neighborhoods, schools, churches, and families—there seems to be no safe refuge from this plague. The issue we're facing isn't any variant of COVID-19, nor of any other known disease. On the surface, the issue we face seems much more benign; much safer than any virological, bacterial, or fungal infection. However, this is much more serious than any epidemic our world has ever faced. The issue we're facing is a serious lack of Christian discipleship.

The hands of men (and viruses) have power only to kill the body, but cannot harm the eternal soul (Matthew 10:28). We should put forth even more effort to protect ourselves from the forces that, through any means possible, seek to spiritually infect us. Spiritual forces are very real, but the way they do battle is far from how we often imagine. The forces of evil whisper pleasant lies and affirmations, slowly drawing attention away from God and onto any number of modern idols. Money, sex, and power are strong motivational categories.[1] If we don't practice proper discipleship, thereby opening the door for the holy renewal of our minds, we'll fall prey, like so many others, to this world's equi-

---

[1] J. Warner Wallace, *Cold-Case Christianity* (Colorado: David C Cook, 2013), 240.

librium (Romans 12:2). I say equilibrium as if I expect it to stay the same. On the contrary, the world is increasingly headed down the wrong path and many will be blindsided by the consequences of how they lived their lives (Matthew 7:21-23).

Speaking of the end times, Jesus said "Because of the increase of wickedness, the love of most will grow cold" (Matthew 24:12). If we have an honest Biblical worldview, it's clear to see that wickedness is increasing at an alarming rate. In fact, the rate itself is increasing at an alarming rate. Now, perhaps more than ever, the church needs to be the church. However, it is abundantly clear that Biblical literacy is a rare attribute. This is by no means a book about the end times, but if we take a good look around us, wickedness is increasing in all directions. Revelation 12:12 tells us there will be a time when the devil is cast out of heaven and his fury will be great because it signals that his reign will soon come to an end. Have we entered that time? Are we approaching the time of Satan's wrath? Time will certainly tell. However, one thing is evident. Christians need to undergo true discipleship. This is our only and most powerful form of warfare against our enemy. Our enemies are not the humans we see, hear, and debate, nor is it the government, nor another nation, nor any earthly anti-Christian organization. Our enemy is the spiritual force whispering sweet lies into their innermost being (Ephesians 6:12).

The Apostle Paul speaks in one of his letters about planting the seed, Apollos watering it and God making it grow (1 Corinthians 3:6). My intention with this book is to take the role of Apollos. If you're one that is seeking to find God, know that this book isn't specifically designed to aid you on that journey. There are many other sources that are much better equipped to help you get that seed planted. Nevertheless, I sincerely hope the words within these pages help to point you in the right direction should

Introduction

you choose to continue here. My intended audience for this book is those that are already professing Christians. I aim to add some water to the plant that has already sprouted and allow God to make it grow. I hope you find, at various times, additional wisdom, knowledge, faith, motivation, encouragement, and the guidance of an impartial third party through your reading. Perhaps most importantly, I hope this book puts that figurative rock in your shoe.

At times throughout this book, I find my own writing crude and unsuitable for civilized conversation. However, I thought it best to include these moments too. Sometimes the issues with which we struggle fall into the crude category and it's worth the discussion. It seems to me that if we were to avoid these topics, we would find ourselves trading righteousness for politeness. Clarity is typically better than ambiguity. Please forgive me when I lead us into discomfort. We'll get through it and hopefully come out just a bit wiser or perhaps a bit stronger in the end.

This book has been divided into three parts. Each part will cover more complex issues than the last. Just as a baby progresses from bland milk to an increased variety of soft solid foods, then finally to the most savory of meats, Christians should focus on fundamentals before seeking to tackle more intricate topics.

In Part One, we'll discuss the basics of the faith: tools to grow in knowledge and relationship with God as well as what Christianity really entails. Included here is a clear presentation of the gospel message. We'll also seek to gain a right understanding of the overwhelming weight of sin and the limitless depths of God's power.

In Part Two, we'll move to the topics of Jesus' true personality and the types of people with which we should spend our time. We'll cover the constant need for introspection and self-adjustment. And perhaps the most difficult subject of Part Two seeks to teach us the importance of mastering the unruliest part of our body, the tongue.

Finally, Part Three will help us understand how, exactly, we are to read the Bible with any sort of accuracy. This section also covers contentment, which is probably my favorite chapter. I truly hope this chapter provides as much help, encouragement, and motivation as I intend. It is certainly not an easy subject. We'll round out Part Three with what I believe is the hardest chapter within this book; hardest both to write as well as to live out. This final chapter is perhaps the culmination of all the other chapters.

This book is *about* discipleship, but is not a *guide to* discipleship. Each chapter handles its own topic and can stand alone. Each topic is important on one's discipleship journey, but there is much more for a follower of Christ to learn. What I mean to say is discipleship doesn't end with this book. Your duty as a Christian is to continue learning and applying God's objective truth to your life and adjusting how you interact with the world around you.

As you read this book, make every effort to place aside all feelings of pride and self-righteousness. Really take a close look at your inner-workings to see where there is room for change or, perhaps, where change is utterly necessary. This is between you and God; the two people that know you better than anyone else. These are also the two people that most want the best for you. And while you may be able to hide from yourself, there is no hiding from God.

Thank you for taking the time to pick up this book and read these words. If you read through the whole thing, thank you all the more. Many hours of prayer have gone into the creation of this book. I hope my writing comes across clear and makes sense in a meaningful way.

Part One

MILK

Part One

MILK

Chapter One
Disciplines of the Faith

"Wax on, wax off. Breathe! In through nose, out the mouth. Wax on, wax off. Don't forget to breathe. Very important. Wax on, wax off." – Mr. Miyagi[1]

As the sun sets, the surroundings within your house grow dimmer and dimmer. Despite having opened all the curtains to harvest every ounce of the scarcely-available rays, it becomes increasingly harder to complete simple tasks and avoid everyday obstacles. Scattered toys quickly change from cluttered nuisance to precarious booby trap. Reading that piece of mail to find out how much you owe on that bill, picking out the right spice and determining the correct amount, choosing the color of socks to match your outfit, and… where was that percentage button again on the keyboard? Oh, that's right. Shift and 5. Without light, life becomes more complicated at best and at times more dangerous.

No one wants to walk in darkness. Except my two-year-old son (at the time of this writing). He loves turning off every light not under direct adult eyesight. He then proceeds to play in the dark, like nothing is even wrong. The darkness may indeed seem

---
[1] John G. Avildsen, *The Karate Kid*. United States: Columbia Pictures, 1984.

fun sometimes, but it presents challenges too. Putting aside the potential hazards of playing in a dark room, we'll also find everything lacks clarity. We may be able to see most things, but we miss the finer details. That Batman's facial expression might not look so cool, we might not be able to find the button on our favorite fire truck, and changing that doll's outfit becomes much more laborious. Perhaps you find yourself in the dark. Maybe you don't even realize how dark it is. You're sitting in your room with the light off, straining to see the toys in your own hands. You need to bring some light to your life! A Christian has three powerful tools for this; reading the Bible, prayer, and fasting. Don't tune me out yet! I'll try to give some easy and practical advice for how to use these effectively. You—yes, I mean you reading this book right now—you can add these tools to your own life in a powerful way and it really won't be as difficult or burdensome as you're probably imagining right now. This is probably the most important chapter in this book!

Bible, prayer, and fasting; to some, this is old news, perhaps even implementing one or more of these tools regularly. If you're in that camp, I encourage you to keep reading anyway. Knowledge is power, right? Many more of us don't utilize these tools as we should. Perhaps you've never been taught how to use them properly. Perhaps your schedule is too busy and you don't see how you can add anything more to your life. Perhaps you've just never cared before and you're trying to do better now. I hope this chapter will encourage people in all situations that you *can* make a change here. Each one of these tools has its place in *your* life and you should learn to use them in the appropriate manner and at the appropriate times.

Just like training at Miyagi-Do, our actions in these areas may not always seem like they'll produce the results we want. However, over time, our mind will adapt to our training. The "wax on, wax off"[2] of regular Bible reading will enable us to reflexively counter falsehoods with the knowledge of Scripture. The "sand the floor"[3] of regular prayer provides strength in times of weakness. The "paint the fence"[4] of periodic fasting provides intense focus to help find clarity, direction, and peace. These skills will improve with use over time, even when we don't see the results we expect on a daily basis.

Read the Bible

Biblical illiteracy is a sad fact of life for the modern church. We have more access to the Bible than any generation in history, yet we know so little of what it actually says. You wouldn't trust a professor you know didn't read any of the class material, yet we often expect people to trust our Biblical knowledge when the last time we touched a Bible was during church at the Christmas service last year. We teach authoritatively on a subject we honestly know little about. "Your word is a lamp to my feet and a light for my path" (Psalm 119:105). That quote from the psalmist, though tired as it may be, is true. We cannot see our path without light. We cannot know God's will for our life if we don't give him the opportunity to speak.

There are many versions of the English Bible and they all vary a bit in length. While there are certainly outliers, I think a fair number is roughly 760,000 words in the Bible for both Old and New Testaments combined.[5] If you read 300 words per minute, that's around 42 hours to read the *entire* Bible. Not to

---

[2] John G. Avildsen, *The Karate Kid*. United States: Columbia Pictures, 1984.
[3] Avildsen, *The Karate Kid*.
[4] Avildsen, *The Karate Kid*.
[5] The Holy Word Church of God, "How Many Words In The Bible," Accessed July 19, 2023, https://holyword.church/miscellaneous-resources/how-many-words-in-the-bible/.

discount the validity of the Old Testament, but the New Testament is more directly applicable to our lives, considerably shorter, often easier to read, and would take just around 10 hours at that same reading speed.

As its title suggests, the Forbes article "Americans Spent On Average More Than 1,300 Hours On Social Media Last Year" claims we spend an exorbitant amount of time just on social media (more than 1,300 hours, to be specific[6]). If we consider the same reading speed we discussed, reading through the New Testament would take less than 1% (roughly 0.77%) of your annual social media time. Can you make that sacrifice? If you were to devote just five minutes per day to reading the New Testament, you would be done in just under four months. Start with that goal. If you're faithful with that, then I bet you'll soon decide to increase that daily time and get done even quicker.

"But wait," you say, "I don't use any social media and I still don't have time to read the Bible." I would assert that you do, indeed, have some time available. Now I know you're thinking I don't know you and your circumstances are different. But do you have a lunch break at work? If you're an hourly employee working a full day, you're usually required to have a thirty-minute lunch break with no work duties allowed. If you're a salaried employee, make that lunch break happen; you have the power. Schools also typically break for lunch for those of us that are students.

What about this one? Do you watch *any* TV? When you read "TV," you should also be thinking Netflix, Hulu, Amazon, Peacock, YouTube, and any of the other myriad streaming plat-

---

[6] Peter Suciu, "Americans Spent On Average More Than 1,300 Hours On Social Media Last Year," June 24, 2021,
https://www.forbes.com/sites/petersuciu/2021/06/24/americans-spent-more-than-1300-hours-on-social-media/?sh=71d3d15c2547.

forms you happen to prefer. Can you make a sacrifice in this area? Many people read recreationally. In fact, you're reading a book right now! Hopefully you're enjoying it so far... So, perhaps you're one of those people that reads for fun. Can you shift a few minutes of your recreational reading to reading the Bible?

Here's another possibility. Yes, we're really going there. I hesitate to bring it up as an option, but do you ever use the toilet? Well, there's your chance; a few minutes of nothing else! Now, before you decide this case is closed, I would feel remiss if I failed to mention my hesitation. Written to the Jews wandering in the desert, Deuteronomy says to do your... business... outside the camp and bury it so the Lord "will not see among you anything indecent and turn away from you" (Deuteronomy 23:14). God made us, and that does, indeed, include everything our bodies excrete. He knows all about the workings of our minds, as well as our bodies. He won't leave you for things your body must do. In fact, the most likely primary function of this rule is health and hygiene. However, I think our modern takeaway is to view our time with God as sacred. We need to approach God with reverence, not flippancy.

The other reason for my hesitation has similar roots in my mind, but regards handwashing. Written for Jews in the same time period, but specifically for the priesthood, was a passage in Exodus: "Whenever they enter the Tent of Meeting, they shall wash with water so that they will not die. Also, when they approach the altar to minister by presenting an offering made to the Lord by fire, they shall wash their hands and feet so that they will not die" (Exodus 30:20-21). This one is specifically for priests, but I make it a habit to wash my hands before my daily reading out of respect. Sometimes it's this simple act that helps ground me and put me in the right mindset to read Scripture. With passages like these, it seems disrespectful to me to read the Bible while on the toilet. However, if this is truly your only time available, I would say you should take the opportunity. But please keep looking for a different timeslot.

If you're still at a loss for a good Bible-reading time, what about your commute to work, school, or to wherever you drive or ride on a regular basis? Turn that time into something truly valuable by getting an audio version of the Bible. This is something I would say isn't ideal, however it's vastly superior to entirely not partaking of the Bible. I say this isn't ideal, but that's not to say I don't think it's a good idea. In fact, I found that I gained a much greater grasp on how the entire Bible fits together when I listened to it straight through for the first time. Since my daily reading is at a much slower pace, that's just something I wasn't able to get by reading it myself. It's much harder for me to get bogged down by a single verse, for example, because it's read one time, then it's immediately on to the next verse. You're free to rewind when you want to hear something again, but I personally loved the fact that it was much harder to stop and dig in. After all, that's what my daily reading is for. It was liberating, in a sense, to just let it play and listen to the entire story of the Bible. It truly gave me a better understanding of the Bible as a whole than my slow-paced daily reading ever did.

I read the Bible every morning. It's the first thing I do, because in my mind, it's putting God first; before everything else in my life. Certainly, things happen from time to time that require me to move my daily reading to a later time slot (kids have a way of changing even the best-made plans), but the majority of days it's first. Set your alarm a few minutes early to accommodate your five-minute-per-day reading plan. Still not convinced to read the Bible every day? That's between you and God, but rather than dismissing it entirely, consider an alternative instead. Can you spend thirty minutes once per week? Fifteen minutes twice per week? These will also bring about a similar timeframe for completion. I'm a strong believer in daily reading, but I think God would be overjoyed if you truly committed to any sort of regular Bible-reading schedule.

My reading schedule nowadays is based less on time or amount read, but the amount that I feel able to really pay attention. Many days that's only one chapter. Sometimes it's five chapters. Regardless of my mental state, I keep one chapter as my minimum. I only choose to read more if my current mental capabilities allow me to focus.

Have you already read the entire Bible? Without use, muscles grow weak. Without study, no expert can stay at the top of his/her field. Things are forgotten. In his letter to the Philippians, Paul says, "It is no trouble for me to write the same things to you again, and it is a safeguard for you" (Philippians 3:1). We need constant reminders. Regardless of how much we know, Peter charges us to "grow in the grace and knowledge of our Lord and Savior Jesus Christ" (2 Peter 3:18). While I'm sure there were Gentiles in Peter's audience, many were Jewish men with formal training in Judaism. These men would have been very familiar with all of the Old Testament Scriptures. Yet Peter doesn't make any exceptions for these men. They, too, are instructed to continue growing in Biblical knowledge.

Paul, again to the Philippians and to us by extension, expresses his desire for the church to increase their knowledge, but goes a step further to give a reason, saying "this is my prayer: that your love may abound more and more in knowledge and depth of insight, so that you may be able to discern what is best and may be pure and blameless until the day of Christ, filled with the fruit of righteousness that comes through Jesus Christ—to the glory and praise of God" (Philippians 1:9-11). Paul managed to fit a lot of meaning in these words. "More in knowledge and depth of insight;" we must read the Scriptures to grow in knowledge, but we are also responsible to use our (God-given) mind to reason and draw insight from our acquired knowledge. Through the accumulation of Biblical knowledge and the diligent application of that knowledge, our "love [will] abound more and more." Through this acquisition and application, we will better "discern what is best" and more fully understand and accept the entirety of Christ's sacrifice and live our lives in a way that is fruitful and does not grieve the Holy Spirit.

I don't remember the source of this analogy (perhaps brilliant apologist, author, speaker, and podcast host, Dr. Frank Turek of crossexamined.org), but I think it illustrates the issue well. Imagine you have a friend. This friend sends you a letter. Being busy with work, you set that letter on a shelf and tell yourself that you'll read it later. Your friend sends another letter. Still busy with kids and friends, it, too, finds its way to the shelf, unread. Again, another letter sent, another letter stored. Letter after letter is piled up, one-by-one, until you have sixty-six unread letters from your friend. One day, unexpectedly, you meet your friend. Your friend tells you how much they've wanted to see you. You, of course, tell your friend how much you missed them and love them. Your friend asks you, "if you love me, why didn't you read my letters?" Of course, your friend in this story is God and the letters he wrote to you are the books of the Bible.

How can I claim to love someone if I refuse to listen to their words? How can I claim someone is good if I don't know the things they've done (or not done)? How can I claim to follow someone if I don't know where they are? How can I claim to speak for someone if I don't know what they say? How can I claim to be a Christian if I don't listen to Christ? Questions such as these helped push me over the edge; from inaction to action. I started and completed a plan to read the entire New Testament in

Disciplines of the Faith

30 days (this is somewhat intense). Immediately following my New Testament completion, I began a plan to read the entire Old Testament in 180 days (this pace is a bit more relaxed). I made it seamlessly through the story sections, but really got bogged down in the laws and genealogies. I ended up slowing way down and not worrying about staying on track to complete it in a certain timeframe. No longer monitoring my progress, I honestly couldn't tell you how long it took. If I were to guess, I'd say probably somewhere in the range of 250-300 days for my Old Testament completion. I say all this simply to illustrate my own various approaches. I began with an intense, focused goal, moved into a less-intense-but-still-focused attitude, then ended with a much more relaxed mindset. None of these are wrong. The only "right" thing is to make it a regular (preferably daily) part of your life.

Without the light shed by God's word, we'll find ourselves stumbling through life. Peter himself would encourage you to read the Bible regularly. He opens the letter of 2 Peter by saying "Grace and peace be yours in abundance through the knowledge of God and of Jesus our Lord" (2 Peter 1:2). The more you read, the more you'll learn, bringing about greater peace in your life (not to be confused with ease of life). Don't be discouraged or overwhelmed by the length of the Bible. In fact, look at the length as a blessing. If it were too short, there wouldn't be enough clarity on many issues we face, nor could we come to adequately understand the nature of God. I'm sure we would also find ourselves bored of reading the same thing repeatedly without a large enough repertoire.

Lastly, James, the (half-) brother of Jesus, exhorts us, "Do not merely listen to the word, and so deceive yourselves. Do what it says" (James 1:22). I'm convinced if we adopt the mentality that we'll put God first by committing to and following through with daily Bible-reading (first thing in the morning!), we'll quickly find ourselves in the right mindset to follow James' advice as well. Focus less on completion and more on the lessons from your daily reading. Give God your firstfruits and enjoy his light in your life.

Pray

Did you know that Jesus has made you a priest? It's true! Check Revelation 1:5-6. We've been ordained to serve God, which includes the privilege of approaching God directly since we're cleansed of sin by the blood of Jesus. With the covering of Jesus' righteousness, we have the ability to convene with the most powerful being in the universe—the master of all creation! See chapter 4 for more on how truly great is God's power.

The writer of Hebrews says, "Therefore, brothers and sisters, since we have confidence to enter the Most Holy Place by the blood of Jesus, by a new and living way opened for us through the curtain, that is, his body, and since we have a great priest over the house of God, let us draw near to God with a sincere heart and with the full assurance that faith brings, having our hearts sprinkled to cleanse us from a guilty conscience and having our bodies washed with pure water" (Hebrews 10:19-22). I realize there are some things here that might not make sense to someone unfamiliar with the Jewish temple and priesthood, but hopefully the message comes through. The Most Holy Place was a room within the temple where God's presence was said to dwell. It was covered by a curtain and the high priest was the only human allowed entry. Furthermore, he was only able to enter one time each year, and that was only after the appropriate ceremonious ongoings. Due solely to Jesus' work, we should have confidence

Disciplines of the Faith

to enter God's presence any time he's present! Spoiler alert: he's always present.

So, we know *that* we are welcome to approach God any time we want. But why *should* we? James says, "The prayer of a righteous man is powerful and effective" (James 5:16). He also says, "You do not have, because you do not ask God" (James 4:2). James is clearly an advocate of an active prayer life. Bring all of your requests to God and they'll be granted!... However, James continues, "When you ask, you do not receive, because you ask with wrong motives, that you may spend what you get on your pleasures" (James 4:3). Motives, then, matter a great deal when it comes to prayer. Financial success in itself is not a bad thing. I often pray that God guides my career and investments. Those are a part of my personal life, so God certainly cares about them and how they affect me. But just because he cares about my career doesn't mean God is obligated to get me a raise or a promotion when I ask for it. Neither must he ensure a huge return on investment if that's my request. God's concern is his kingdom. Souls. If my financial success contributes to building God's kingdom, he may grant my request.

In prayer, a focus on character development and relationships is much more important than financial success. Pray that you will gain an increasing measure of "love, joy, peace, patience, kindness, goodness, faithfulness, gentleness and self-control" (Galatians 5:22-23). James mentions wisdom, "If any of you lacks wisdom, he should ask God, who gives generously to all without finding fault, and it will be given to him" (James 1:5). James continues with a large caveat, "But when he asks, he must believe and not doubt, because he who doubts is like a wave of the sea, blown and tossed by the wind. That man should not think he will receive anything from the Lord; he is a double-minded man, unstable in all he does" (James 1:6-8). In other words, you must not only ask for the right things, but you must also trust in God's ability to grant those things. We develop skill in prayer through regular use and as we gain knowledge of the Bible to better understand how to pray.

Let's review a story from Abraham's life. In Genesis 18:20-32, we see some dialogue between Abraham and God. The Lord had visited Abraham and was on his way to Sodom (and Gomorrah) to destroy it for its wickedness. You remember the destruction of Sodom and Gomorrah, with the woman looking back and turning to a pillar of salt, right? You may also remember that Abraham's nephew, Lot (the salt-woman's husband), lived in Sodom. Hearing of his nephew's imminent danger undoubtedly caused some panic for Abraham. Abraham asked God if he would spare the city if there were fifty righteous people. God said if he found fifty righteous people in the city, he would spare it. Abraham asked again if God would spare the city for forty-five righteous people, and God consented. The cycle continued, with Abraham asking to spare the city for forty, thirty, twenty, and finally ten righteous people. God agreed to each request, patiently allowing Abraham to reach a point with which he was satisfied. We can ask God for whatever we want, but we mustn't expect God to answer a particular way just because it's what we want.

Notice Abraham's attitude throughout the conversation. Abraham, the "exalted father" of many nations, seemed timid! "Now that I have been so bold as to speak to the Lord, though I am nothing but dust and ashes" (Genesis 18:27), and "May the Lord not be angry, but let me speak" (Genesis 18:30), and "Now that I have been so bold as to speak to the Lord" (Genesis 18:31), and finally "May the Lord not be angry, but let me speak just once more" (Genesis18:32). Abraham's demeanor is a lesson in itself. Notice how he prefaces his requests. Beyond his demeanor, we can learn more from this interaction. Abraham recognized his

Disciplines of the Faith

place and God's authority, while also understanding God's goodness and expecting God to do what was right, saying "Will not the Judge of all the earth do right?" (Genesis 18:25).

Abraham took the initiative to ask God to do what he (Abraham) thought was right, while understanding that God was going to do the right thing, *even if* the right thing wasn't what Abraham thought it was. It's also very important to note that even though Abraham already expected God to do the right thing, he still asked; he still brought the request to the Lord. We're expected to speak with God through prayer. As we'll see through Daniel's story later in this chapter, sometimes God waits for us to pray before acting. So, we should come to God with the confidence that comes through knowing that he wants us to make our requests. Although we must also remember that God will do what is right, regardless of what we *think* is right. In chapter 10, we'll spend a bit of time addressing the issue of pain and times in which it doesn't seem to us that God does what is right.

Normal things are, well… normal. Did that statement just shake the core of your being? Doubtful. We know that the ordinary is ordinary; natural is natural. We hear of God and all of the power he wields. We read stories in the Bible of all the times he worked outside the realm of normal and ordinary. After hearing of these powerful events, we sometimes, whether consciously or unconsciously, fall under the belief that God often works in miraculous ways. On the contrary, God tends to work in mundane ways. He uses natural events, rather than supernatural. Of course, God certainly has the ability to work through supernatural means. However, as the creator of the natural world, why would God want to supersede his own order with regularity? What novelist or screenwriter would want to repeatedly overrule the world of their own creation? Perhaps at a climactic moment, working outside the bounds of their world could bring special excitement to the viewer, but that would have to be a rare exception or else the audience will no longer be invested; they'll no longer care about the consequences of any actions taken by the hero or the villain. Without the threat of real, lasting consequences, nothing has any significance.

Wait a second. Isn't the Bible full of miracles? While the definitive number is debated for various reasons, one source counts 163 miracles in the Bible: eighty-three in the Old Testament and eighty in the New Testament.[7] This may sound like a lot, but let's put a bit more perspective in the mix. While the exact period of time will vary depending on whom you ask, the Bible covers roughly 4,000 years of history. If we just do some simple math, that averages to about one miracle every twenty-four years. That's even rounding down. In other words, even in the Bible—the Holy Book, the book that aims to give us what we need to seek, find, and serve God—even in this book, miracles are not an everyday occurrence. In fact, at the rate of our calculation, there's only an average of around four per century. What were you doing twenty-four years ago? Twenty-four years between miracles truly is a long gap in supernatural activity from this God we expect to intervene in a miraculous way any time we come with a request.

The issue compounds itself when we consider that miracles tend to be grouped around a particular event. Twenty of the Old Testament miracles were centered around the life of Moses and the liberation of the Israelites and deliverance to the future land of Israel just in the book of Exodus. They were designed to teach the Israelites of God's power and that Moses was speaking by God's authority. And this doesn't even include the miracles

---

[7] Staff, "How Many Miracles Are There In The Bible?" February 28, 2019, https://www.spiritoflifeag.com/how-many-miracles-are-there-in-the-bible/.

around Moses' life aimed at this same goal that are in other books; the book of Numbers contains another seven, for example. The entire New Testament was centered around the coming of God in human flesh and affirming certain people as teaching by God's authority.

When we consider these groupings, our average amount of time between miracles grows considerably. If the Old Testament covers around 3,500 years and we exclude twenty-nine miracles surrounding Israel's journey from slavery in Egypt to the Promised Land, there are fifty-four miracles left to spread out; about one every sixty-five years. We can continue this trend. Several miracles surrounded Elijah and Elisha, for example. Are we to conclude, then, that God isn't working in all the years there are no miracles? Absolutely not! So, just what kind of work is he doing in all those non-miracle years? God is working within the ordinary forces we take for granted. Rather than breaking the divinely fine-tuned rules of his own creation, he uses natural forces to create the outcomes he desires. We might end up with more money in our bank account than we thought possible. We might get done with a school or work project faster than we thought we could. Perhaps our loved one was able to recover from an illness in which we didn't think they would survive. This list can go on and on to include every request we might ever bring to God in prayer.

God could absolutely use miracles to accomplish any of these feats, however he is more likely to use aspects of his own creation to enact his will. In chapter 10, we'll discuss the ripple effect and how small, seemingly insignificant, natural things can have life-altering impacts. There are most certainly miracles that happened in Biblical times that aren't recorded in the Bible. John even says this at the end of his Gospel (John 21:25). The point is that miracles are not common events. We need to look for the ways our sovereign God acts within the rules that he set for the universe. Didn't get hit by that speeding car whose driver insisted on sending a text message at that moment? Maybe God allowed some trash to blow in front of them, slowing them down just enough to avoid a collision (perhaps even miles earlier). In fact, you might not even have any idea that God was answering your prayer to provide you with safe travel because the collision *didn't* happen. This is just one example of what might as well be infinite possibilities of how our all-powerful God works within the bounds he set for the natural world. We mustn't allow a lack of supernatural /miracles to deter us from approaching God.

What's the most important component of literally every human relationship that has ever existed? Communication. Think otherwise? Perhaps you're thinking of a relationship that doesn't use spoken or written words. Perhaps two people brought together in a survival situation or even a prison cell don't speak the same language, but a strong bond can still be formed. Communication goes far beyond simple spoken or written words. We use the term "body language" for a reason. We can gather much about how a person is feeling and even convey concern and empathy with nothing but our body or facial expressions. This, too, is communication, albeit not necessarily as sophisticated as spoken language. But body language often excels at communicating things we simply don't know how to express adequately in words.

The paradigm of nonverbal communication has to be Helen Keller. As you quite possibly know, Keller was blind and deaf. She lost both of these senses at the age of only 19-months-old. Despite having no sight or hearing, Keller was able to write many books and essays. How was she able to learn written language when she couldn't see or hear? Using her sense of touch alone, Keller's teacher taught her how to read and write. On a level that's much more relatable to most of us, think about a young child that has yet to develop the ability to produce full thoughts with words. The child certainly has thoughts, opinions, and emotions, and often the parents understand many of these things despite the child's inability to verbally articulate them.

So, why bring up non-wordy language when we're supposed to be talking about prayer? Sometimes prayer itself can feel overwhelming; we simply feel lost in what we should even pray about. This is especially true for those of us without a history of regular prayer, however it's also true of those with devout prayer lives. At times, life seems to be falling apart in so many places, all we can think to do when we try to pray is just sit in silence, feeling helpless. Even in these times, our prayer is important.

On my hour-long commute to work every morning, I pray. Many times, I'm able to speak openly, frankly, and abundantly. Sometimes my words are very few and my thoughts and worries are far too many. In these times, it helps to remember the Holy Spirit works to fill in the gaps for us: "We do not know what we ought to pray for, but the Spirit himself intercedes for us with groans that words cannot express. And he who searches our hearts knows the mind of the Spirit, because the Spirit intercedes for the saints in accordance with God's will" (Romans 8:26-27). A child's groans are able to express things to their parents when they don't know the words to say. Words are not always adequate to express our true feelings and desires, but God picks up the slack. We just have to make the effort.

And just to offer one last nugget of comfort here, Jesus said, "When you pray, do not keep on babbling like pagans, for they think they will be heard because of their many words. Do not be like them, for your Father knows what you need before you ask him" (Matthew 6:7-8). God knows what we need before we even think to pray (see chapter 4 for more on God's omniscience), so do your best with wording and let God fill in the gaps. In fact, we can even add that request in our prayer! Be open and honest with God. After all, he already knows our weaknesses. Additionally, we sometimes listen to people pray and they're just able to spit out word after word, leaving us with feelings of inadequacy over our own meager word count in our typical prayers. Don't focus on number of words or length of prayer. Pray for the right things with the right heart and you'll be just fine.

Now that we're hopefully a bit less intimidated by prayer, how, exactly, should we pray? Jesus gives a model prayer for us, commonly known as the Lord's Prayer. Most of us that have it memorized use old language like from the King James Version: "Our Father which art in heaven, Hallowed be thy name. Thy kingdom come. Thy will be done in earth, as it is in heaven. Give us this day our daily bread. And forgive us our debts, as we forgive our debtors. And lead us not into temptation, but deliver us from evil: For thine is the kingdom, and the power, and the glory, for ever. Amen" (Matthew 6:9-13 KJV). Let's break down Jesus' model prayer, but we'll use a more modern telling this time.

Disciplines of the Faith

Jesus' prayer	What it means for us
"Our Father in heaven, hallowed be your name," (Matthew 6:9)	God, you are far above me in heaven and you are holy. This is praise for God.
"your kingdom come, your will be done on earth as it is in heaven." (Matthew 6:10)	Let everything be as you desire it to be. You know far better than me what is best for me, those around me, and the world as a whole.
"Give us today our daily bread." (Matthew 6:11)	Please provide for my needs today and perhaps even some of my wants.
"Forgive us our debts, as we also have forgiven our debtors." (Matthew 6:12)	We all make mistakes. Please forgive me when I mess up. And please give me the mental and emotional fortitude to do the same for all of the other flawed humans in my life.
"And lead us not into temptation, but deliver us from the evil one." (Matthew 6:13)	Temptation is everywhere (especially nowadays). Please help me to avoid falling into the trap of sin.

Fast

Does every day present the same level of stress? Does every season of life offer the same amount of difficulty? Does every test, relationship, conversation, or financial burden have the same effect on us? Of course not. Situations are different and therefore place differing levels of burden on us financially, mentally, emotionally, and physically. Every day is not the same, nor is every season in our lives. Some months are harder than others.

Some years are more difficult. Sometimes tough seasons can even last a decade or more.

As any American can tell you, there is a season for football. During the 18-week NFL playing season, players are certainly expected to train physically and mentally. Much of the hard work, however, is actually performed in the off-season. NFL teams have a nine-week program to prepare for the upcoming playing season. The nine weeks have to follow a specified regimen, during which the teams are prohibited from certain types of training. In the final phase of the program, coaches are allowed to hold a three-day mandatory minicamp. These minicamps are typically geared toward preparing the newer players for what's to come in the approaching playing season as well as what to expect from their new career in the NFL. There are currently thirty-two teams in the NFL. In the 2022 season, thirty coaches held mandatory minicamps; only two did not.[8] Those non-mandatory minicamp teams are Cincinnati and Philadelphia for anyone that's curious. Since the overwhelming majority of NFL teams hold mandatory minicamps, it's safe to assume there is much perceived value in the additional training, even though it's only up to three days.

Fasting is a tool to be used in much the same way. Think of it as your minicamp to prepare you for an upcoming trial. When we see trouble approaching, that's an excellent time to fast. Even if we're currently in the midst of our playing season, it may be time for such a minicamp to get us back on the right track. Minicamps are typically three-days long, however fasting need not be that length of time. Fasting can be three days or one day

---

[8] "NFL offseason workout program dates announced for all 32 teams ahead of 2022 NFL season," National Football League, April 1, 2022, www.nfl.com/_amp/nfl-offseason-workout-program-dates-announced-ahead-of-2022-season-for-all-32-te.

or even twelve hours. We're the head coach and can set the length of our own minicamp based on how much training our team needs.

      Why is fasting a useful tool? When utilized properly, fasting is powerful. It can help strengthen us mentally and emotionally. It can lead to greater spiritual insight than we previously possessed. However, these things don't come from simply a lack of eating. On the contrary, we must do more than abstain from food if we want our minicamp to be successful. When we fast, we should use the time we would have spent preparing (or procuring) and consuming food instead on the other disciplines we discussed earlier in this chapter. When we would normally be cooking or driving to the restaurant or scrolling through our DoorDash app, we should turn instead to the Bible. We can perhaps find a section that speaks about that with which we're currently struggling. The New Testament is filled with a wealth of practical advice on daily living. The Psalms can provide great comfort knowing that some of the greatest "heroes of the faith" struggled with the same doubts and hardships we face today. Reflect on your reading and spend time in prayer.

Conclusion

"The kingdom of heaven is like treasure hidden in a field. When a man found it, he hid it again, and then in his joy went and sold all he had and bought that field. Again, the kingdom of heaven is like a merchant looking for fine pearls. When he found one of great value, he went away and sold everything he had and bought it" (Matthew 13:44-46). Notice the major similarity here. In both of Jesus' parables, the person found something of enormous value and sold everything they had in order to buy it. Can you imagine that; trading everything you own for one single thing? We don't know the profession of man 1, but man 2 is a merchant. That indicates that this man most likely had a fairly high net worth. Yet both men chose to forsake everything they owned to gain the one thing they found of greater value. This is what the kingdom of heaven is like. Beloved author and apologist C. S. Lewis famously said, "Christianity is a statement which, if false, is of no importance, and, if true, of infinite importance. The one thing it cannot be is moderately important."[9] I can't think of a better way to say it than that. But let's try to rephrase it so the point might come across. If Christianity is not true, then following it or not following it has no bearing on your eternal soul whatsoever. However, if Christianity is true, there is no treasure buried in a field, no fine pearl... no job, no car, no spouse, no friend, no video game, no night out, no education, no clothes, no addiction—there is *nothing* more important to you than Christianity. And that's true whether you believe in Christianity or not because truth does not require belief.

Jesus followed these metaphors of the kingdom with this more somber picture: "Once again, the kingdom of heaven is like a net that was let down into the lake and caught all kinds of fish. When it was full, the fishermen pulled it up on the shore. Then they sat down and collected the good fish in baskets, but threw the bad away. This is how it will be at the end of the age. The angels will come and separate the wicked from the righteous and throw them into the fiery furnace, where there will be weeping and gnashing of teeth" (Matthew 13:47-50). As we'll discuss in chapter 10, all things will be made right. This includes healing for the wrongs done to God's people, but it also includes "weeping and gnashing of teeth" for those that do not belong to God.

---

[9] C. S. Lewis, "Christian Apologetics," *God in the Dock*, edited by Walter Hooper. (Michigan: Wm. B. Eerdmans Publishing Co., 2014), 102.

Don't be a bad fish. Jesus' return will be dreadful, indeed, for those that don't know him.

Jesus also said "Many will say to me on that day, 'Lord, Lord, did we not prophesy in your name, and in your name drive out demons and perform many miracles?' Then I will tell them plainly, 'I never knew you. Away from me, you evildoers!'" (Matthew 7:22-23). I imagine that's the beginning of their weeping and gnashing of teeth. It would be absolutely horrible to be in that situation! But Jesus tells us it will happen to *many* people. That means there are *many* people in the church that do not truly belong to Jesus. Are you one of these people? Paul tells us to "Examine yourselves to see whether you are in the faith; test yourselves" (2 Corinthians 13:5). Don't continue to deceive yourself. Honestly examine your life, actions, and priorities. Once you have an honest assessment, take action to grow closer to Jesus so his return will be the best moment of your life.

Whether we are currently a good fish or a bad fish, the solution to a closer walk with Jesus is likely the same. Use these pillars of discipleship to learn and grow. First and foremost, read the Bible. With greater knowledge and understanding of Scripture (along with pure motivations), we'll grow closer to God. I know it doesn't always sound fun to read a document that's around 2,000-or-more years-old, but I find the more time that I read the Bible when I *don't* want to, the more I have a desire to actually read the Bible in the long run. Perhaps some people that exercise regularly can relate. You may not always feel like exercising, but if you bite the bullet and do it, then you often *want* to do it.

Secondly, have an active prayer life. Communication is the basis of every relationship. Do your best to communicate your praise, repentance, needs, and wants and know that the Holy Spirit will intercede for you. God already knows it all in intricate detail. All you have to do is make the good faith attempt to communicate.

And finally, utilize fasting <u>in conjunction</u> with Bible-reading and prayer. I would assert that fasting without study or prayer is useless. A major purpose of fasting is to free up time for these other things. If I fast, my meal times become study and prayer times; usually a bit of both for each session, rather than one or the other. In Daniel 10, we see a time of fasting and intense prayer in the life of the prophet Daniel. He was struggling with understanding a vision he was given. For three weeks, Daniel "ate no choice food; no meat or wine touched [his] lips; and [he] used no lotions at all" (Daniel 10:3). It also implies that Daniel engaged in intense prayer (and probably study) during this time of fasting. Daniel's period of fasting, prayer, and study, coincided with the exact period of time an angel was engaged in spiritual warfare. The angel told Daniel his prayer was heard and the answer was sent immediately, however the angel was detained for the three weeks. Thus, Daniel's answer arrived twenty-one days later. I find this passage particularly interesting because it offers us a glimpse into the spiritual world. This story from Daniel's life is an excellent example to us.

When we face trials in life, we must remember to be persistent in our application of these foundational disciplines. In Luke 18:1-8, Jesus tells us a parable of a widow persistently seeking justice. The widow incessantly seeks justice from a judge that cares nothing for her, for justice, or for God. The judge refuses at first, but over time, he's worn down by the widow's consistency. Eventually, the judge grants the widow's request due solely to her persistence in asking, saying "I will see that she gets justice, so that she won't eventually wear me out with her coming!" (Luke 18:5). Jesus follows the parable by saying "Listen to what the unjust judge says. And will not God bring about justice for his chosen ones, who cry out to him day and night? Will he keep putting them off? I tell you, he will see that they get justice, and quickly. However, when the Son of Man comes, will he find faith on the earth?" (Luke 18:6-8). Jesus is inviting us here to be persistent in asking for the right things in prayer. God undoubtedly cares much more for our requests than an unjust judge. But Jesus also echoes (actually Jesus' teaching came first) the passage from James we discussed earlier. We must believe when we ask or else we should not expect a response (James 1:6-8).

Use the tools at your disposal. You may be aiding an angel that's been sent to carry your answer to you. We're locked in this physical world and we often forget there's much more to creation than what we see. Paul reminds us that our enemies are not those that we see—our rivals, neighbors, critics, or our bosses. Our true enemies are the dark, spiritual forces that rule this world (Ephesians 6:12). We must faithfully and consistently fulfill our duty in this spiritual war.

Chapter Two
Faith Saves

"It is finished." – Jesus[1]

    I'll often hear of stories in which people feel they're beyond saving. They think there's no possible way that God would ever forgive them for what they've done. Perhaps even you're in that same boat. Well, there's definitely one thing we can both agree on there. You certainly are evil (see chapter 7). And I don't even know what you've done! Where our thoughts may differ is in your save-ability. You can be saved. The ball is completely in your court, however the power absolutely does not lie with you. Your evilness can indeed be forgiven by God if you truly wish for it. Although the context is different, it's still applicable to point out that Jesus said "you are worth more than many sparrows" (Matthew 10:31). Still not onboard with my thinking? Let's turn our attention to the life of a young Jewish man named Saul.
    Our Saul was likely named after Saul, the first king of Israel. Young Saul was a member of a highly-esteemed Jewish sect and

---

[1] John 19:30

studied under a respected teacher. Saul poured his life into his Jewish studies and was zealous for his Jewish faith from a young age. When followers of a religious cult began popping up all over the place, spreading what Saul knew to be lies that would mislead the masses, Saul knew they had to be stopped. Threats of legal action didn't seem to deter these religious zealots. It was clear to Saul that something more drastic had to be done. Saul began targeting members of this heretical faith, going door-to-door to people's homes to take them to prison, even going so far as approving of mob violence and murder. Young Saul wasn't content keeping his actions within his own city, so he sought and obtained official approval from those in authority to take his violent retribution to another town.

While on the way to the next town, Saul had a conversion experience in which Jesus told him to seek out and speak with a certain Christian. Saul met the man and "officially" became a Christian. This Saul, persecutor and murderer of Christians, became a Christian. However, Saul didn't just become any run-of-the-mill Christian. Saul is better known to us as Paul, the Apostle. If you're familiar enough with the Bible, you may know that the authorship of about half of the New Testament documents are attributed to this same Paul. Paul was undoubtedly one of the greatest evangelists of his time and his words have reached nearly 2,000 years into the future to affect and teach Christians throughout all of the Christian church's subsequent history. God not only forgave Saul of his grave, murderous sins, but he also gave him a new identity and even a new name. This man went from Saul, persecutor and murderer of God's people to Paul, the Apostle of Christ. You *can* be forgiven. Will you humble yourself before God and allow him to direct you on your path of repentance?

Faith Alone: No Works Required

How good must one be in order to earn salvation? How do you measure up to that standard? Will you be able to meet that standard before you die? Let's go ahead and jump straight to those answers. You must be perfect to earn salvation. You don't come close by any measure of that perfect standard. You will never be able to attain the standard of perfection on this side of eternity. Just in case you're still holding out hope that you can somehow meet this standard of perfection, let me remind you that you have already sinned. You are already blemished. Perfection, then, cannot be attained. Even if you're somehow able to never sin again, you cannot be perfect because you are already imperfect. Your record is already tarnished.

Does this mean to imply that no one will spend eternity with God? We are indeed all sinners and unable to measure up to God's moral standard (Romans 3:23). "There is no one righteous, not even one" (Romans 3:10). We are all in need of a savior. We stand guilty in the courtroom of God. God cannot let us go free, because his infinite justice must be satisfied. In conflict with his infinite justice is his infinite mercy. The price for sin must be paid, but God wants to forgive the sinner. In order to accomplish both his justice and his mercy, he sent the second member of the Trinity, Jesus, to have our sins placed upon his perfect shoulders and God's wrath was poured out upon him in our place.

"If you confess with your mouth, 'Jesus is Lord,' and believe in your heart that God raised him from the dead, you will be saved" (Romans 10:9). Once we truly make this commitment, not only do we give our sins to Jesus, but he actually attributes his righteousness to us. This is why the gospel is so often called the good news. Our salvation doesn't rely on our ability to be perfect or earn our way into heaven. No human can ever live up to God's perfect moral standard. This is an enormous burden (infinite, in fact) that God himself lifted from our shoulders! There is no more hard work to be done. Just confess and believe. We are saved by grace, through faith. God provides the grace when we put our faith in Jesus. This is the gospel message. This is most excellent news, indeed.

Works Must Be Present

Just when we've convinced ourselves that faith is all that's required of us in order to gain eternal salvation, here's a nasty little wrench. James, the half-brother of Jesus, says "Show me your faith without deeds, and I will show you my faith by what I do" (James 2:18). James chapter 2 even gives some Biblical examples of people "considered righteous" for their deeds. So, is our salvation situation in reality more complex than we just determined in the previous section? Spoiler alert: nope.

The book of James gives us some really practical wisdom we can apply to our everyday lives. Likewise, James' teaching about works being a necessary part of the process is very wise. Unfortunately, this argument that, at a surface level, seems to conflict with Paul's "grace through faith" assertion, has led many to misunderstand and believe it's their own works that save them. In fact, in *Letter to the American Church*, Eric Metaxas devotes a good amount of writing to describe Martin Luther's struggle with the faith versus works "contradiction." Martin Luther, of course, was a key figure of the Protestant Reformation. He's the nailer the famous (or perhaps infamous, in some eyes) Ninety-Five Theses that is often thought of as the beginning of the Reformation. In the end, Luther was able to reconcile the two teachings and understand the complementary dynamic between the two.[2]

---

[2] Eric Metaxas, *Letter to the American Church* (Washington, D.C.: Salem Books, 2022), 55-60.

When we more closely examine James' point, we see his teaching is actually complementary, rather than contradictory, to Paul's. James' final statement in his "faith and works" section sums up his entire point. "As the body without the spirit is dead, so faith without deeds is dead" (James 2:26). As we already determined through Paul's teaching, we're saved as a result of our faith and no amount of works can ever justify us before God. We can never measure up to God's standard or earn our way to salvation. James' entire point is that works are a necessary outcome of genuine faith. You cannot have a genuine conversion and live a life that does not produce good fruit. To turn that double-negative sentence into a positive statement, if you have a genuine conversion, you will live a life that produces good fruit. You will exhibit good works. If you claim to have faith, but have no good works, James says you're no better than the demons who also believe God exists, and shudder (James 2:19). It is possible to intellectually believe that God exists without putting our trust—our faith—in him. If our faith—our trust in God with our eternal salvation—is genuine, good works will result out of our love for and appreciation of God's forgiveness of our sins.

What constitutes good works? There are way too many possibilities to list! God's law is written on our hearts (Romans 2:15), so we should already have a good idea of some of the good we can do. Of course, it would be foolish of us to think we can do just *any* good work. Just because we're good at something, doesn't mean that's something we should necessarily do. In fact, we may hate that thing, despite our skill. On the contrary, we may absolutely love another thing with which we're not so good. We're all unique creations and have our own place in the body of Christ. We're all individuals with our own mix of gifts and talents and knowledge and preferences with which the Lord has blessed us. Look for those good works that intersect with these traits. Paul says we combine all of these aspects to serve in various ways that best fit who we are. "If a man's gift is prophesying, let him use it in proportion to his faith. If it is serving, let him serve; if it is teaching, let him teach; if it is encouraging, let him encourage; if it is contributing to the needs of others, let him give generously; if it is leadership, let him govern diligently; if it is showing mercy, let him do it cheerfully" (Romans 12:6-8). This is certainly not meant to be an all-inclusive list. Paul gives us several categories as examples. Within each category, lies countless specific possibilities for individual works.

We must look for the opportunities that fit us in all our uniqueness, but be open to uncomfortable situations at times. The Bible has many examples of God's call to good works upon those who did not want to do so. Sometimes the recipient of the command was insecure and felt unqualified for the work. We're looking at you, Moses (Exodus 4:10-13). However, the prime example that comes to mind is Jonah's story. God told Jonah to go to Nineveh to preach against it.

Nineveh was a large city that housed all sorts of evil practices. Jonah didn't want to warn the city of God's impending judgment because he didn't want them to repent and be saved. Doesn't this sound like us sometimes? Rather than following God's direct command to go to Nineveh, Jonah got on a boat headed in the opposite direction. However, God wouldn't be deterred by something so trivial. He stirred up the sea, so that the sailors feared for their lives. When they asked Jonah what they needed to do to save themselves, Jonah instructed them to throw him overboard. And this is where the famous fish comes in! A "great fish" swallowed Jonah, sent courtesy of God (Jonah 1:17). If this is how God would run a rideshare service, I think I'd rather take my chances with Lyft or Uber.

You know the next part of the story. Three days in the belly of the fish and he was spit back out onto dry land. Finally in Nineveh, Jonah began to work his way through the city, preaching the message God sent him to proclaim. This should have been a three-day tour due to the size of the city, but Jonah's message, delivered with halfhearted, lukewarm fervor, caused a massive shift throughout the city in only one day. The entire city, from the animals to the king, fasted, prayed, and put on sackcloth—an itchy, inelegant material that helped in this case to demonstrate a humble and submissive demeanor toward God.

Jonah's story has a lot of lessons we can learn, even beyond what we're looking at here. Most specifically to our topic, Jonah was obviously a gifted preacher. He spoke so powerfully that he only needed to reach one third of the city with his message in order for the entire population to repent. That's one impactful speaker! If God calls someone to do something, regardless of how that person feels about their ability to perform the task, know that the person is fully equipped to complete the job exactly as God intends. Jonah completed his three-day mission in a single day, but throw on top of that the fact that it's not even something he wanted to do. His heart wasn't in it. Yet he succeeded, nonetheless. Sometimes Christians must do things they really don't want to do in order to follow God. Sometimes God has prepared us with the skills we need to perform a good work, but the passion for that task isn't there. The first thing to enter my mind as I write that last sentence is all of the martyrs throughout the church's history. I'm sure what they did would be considered good works, however I have no doubt they would rather not have had to go to their deaths—often involving torture.

So, how do we transform this works business into some practical advice for the life of the typical American Christian? Give money to your church or another good cause. Please prioritize your church when making donations. Your pastor needs to be paid. If there is a building, there are expenses involved in that upkeep. If your church has enough money, it can be used to benefit other causes or to aid in community outreach efforts or for future growth. Perhaps you have extra time. Use that time to volunteer with your church (Remember that building upkeep?), or a homeless shelter, or a nursing home, or that neighbor that's not physically capable of yard work anymore, or any number of other places that people need help getting things done or just need someone with whom to speak. Perhaps you have some sort of platform or leadership role with which you can speak openly about Jesus. Or maybe you just take the opportunity to speak about Jesus with any individual when the chance arises.

Remember chapter 1? Reading the Bible, prayer, and fasting can all be good works, although in themselves, they're more inwardly-focused and we probably need to exhibit some other good works alongside those basics. Jonah likely spent a great deal of time doing these things, but that didn't stop God from sending him to Nineveh. Jesus told two very similar parables, one about talents (Matthew 25:14-30) and the other about minas (Luke 19:12-27). Let's focus on Luke's story.

A man left home and gave a mina (an amount of money) to each of his servants with the instruction to "Put this money to work" (Luke 19:13). The expectation, of course, would be for each servant to use that money to make more money. When the man returned home, he called his servants together. It was time for them to account for the work they had done in their master's absence. One servant used the mina to earn an additional ten minas. The next used their provided mina to earn another five. Both were clearly successful with their missions and they were awarded leadership over ten and five cities, respectively.

The last servant came and gave the one mina back to his master, saying he had kept it hidden away the entire time because he didn't want to risk losing the money. The master was angry with this servant and took the mina from him after a scolding. Presumably, this man was subsequently killed with the other mutinous servants (Luke 19:27), just as was the lazy servant in Matthew's story (Matthew 25:30). The lazy servants were given gifts to use to further the master's purposes. They chose to not take any risks with their gifts. More than that, they chose to not even take the easy road of putting the money into a bank to earn a measly, but secure amount of interest (Matthew 25:27; Luke 19:23). The Bible doesn't specify, but I would bet if one of those servants had lost their allotted money in an honestly well-intentioned manner, the master would have forgiven them for at least trying. They may not have partaken in any reward for their failure, but they would have avoided the punishment nonetheless.

Aim for Gold

Have you ever participated in a race or been a member of a sports team? Perhaps you even competed in a lot of sports when you were in school. What about other types of tournaments or competitions? There are card tournaments, music competitions, dancing, cooking, debate, art, and the list goes on. When you participated in any of these events, did you ever hope to lose? Surely not. On the contrary, we hope to win! We certainly may understand we really have no chance of winning, but the desire is still there. The effort we invest in the game/match/round is still there in the hope of victory. Sometimes it's just the opposite—we see no chance whatsoever of losing, yet we sometimes find ourselves snatching defeat from the jaws of victory. Perhaps we stopped putting in the effort to win in the last few seconds, thinking there's no way they could make that three-pointer, or they can't possibly run the ball seventy yards, or it's impossible for them to make it past our fullback and goalie with the time remaining.

Fortunately, we're on the winning team and there is absolutely no chance that the opposing side can steal our victory. God's team is victorious and all of our teammates will be rewarded with the crown of eternal life (James 1:12). That is one valuable trophy! It's a prize that everyone should strive to obtain. In fact, it's the most important prize we can ever win. Without it, we're on the losing side of this game; this most serious and weighty game. Regardless of how lofty are our athletic or academic achievements—no matter what level of any championship in which we have ever competed—there has never been a more prestigious prize for winning, nor a graver consequence for losing. And it's Jesus, our coach and star player, that brings about our resounding victory.

Even though we know that victory is in the bag, we're not exempted from contributing to the team. We can't just show up to the championship game, walk out onto the court, and sit down for forty-eight minutes. Well, I guess we *could*, but I don't think our coach would be happy with us. We would be just like the mina-burying servant from the previous section. If we truly cared about the game, our coach, and our team, we wouldn't just show up to the game. We would go onto the court and for the entire forty-eight minutes, we would give every ounce of strength we have to achieve victory. This intense effort, naturally, takes effort. I know that's redundant, but it's an important statement. Far too often, we coast; just resting on our star player to do all of the work. We went so far as to join the team, but we didn't join to be all-stars. We want the benefit of winning with none of the work.

Faith Saves

Paul uses a sports analogy, saying, "Do you not know that in a race all the runners run, but only one gets the prize? Run in such a way as to get the prize" (1 Corinthians 9:24). Ricky Bobby might repeat the words of his father, "If you ain't first, you're last."[3] Of course, we know that this advice is false. We also know that we don't have to be the best Christian to have ever lived in order to receive the prize of eternal life. There are no limits on the number of rooms in God's house. But we still must try. We need to not only show up to the game, but we need to play hard—like the championship depends on it—like our coach and teammates are counting on us to play our position well.

In addition to being awarded the crown of life simply for being a genuine part of Jesus' team, every true believer will receive other rewards; and they won't be equal. We will all be rewarded justly for our works. "For we must all appear before the judgment seat of Christ, that each one may receive what is due him for the things done while in the body, whether good or bad" (2 Corinthians 5:10). Remember the story of the minas? The one who used his talents, desires, opportunities, etc. to his utmost ability was put in charge of ten cities. The one who used his talents, desires, opportunities, etc. to a large extent was put in charge of five cities. And, of course, the one that squandered all that he was given was not placed in charge of any cities. On the contrary, he had his gifts removed from him.

Let's consider Jesus' words, "That servant who knows his master's will and does not get ready or does not do what his master wants will be beaten with many blows. But the one who does not know and does things deserving punishment will be beaten with few blows. From everyone who has been given much, much

---

[3] Adam McKay, *Talladega nights: The Ballad of Ricky Bobby*. United States: Columbia Pictures, 2006.

will be demanded; and from the one who has been entrusted with much, much more will be asked" (Luke 12:47-48). This sure sounds like one of those "ignorance is bliss" moments to me! The more we know or the more God has given us—of public platform, money, education—of wisdom, knowledge, skill, courage, strength, endurance, discernment, understanding, hope, love, patience—the more we have been given, the more that God expects of us. At first glance, this seems like a situation we'd be crazy to embrace. However, it's actually a massive privilege. If the God of "life, the universe, and everything"[4] bestows upon us those traits we need to complete his work—to be a strong, central part of his team; if he gives us enormous potential in terms of talent, ability, and opportunity, then we know that he trusts us to use those gifts well. He knows us better than we know ourselves.

When Moses protested his divine appointment, thinking he wasn't good enough, God said, "Who gave man his mouth? Who makes him deaf or mute? Who gives him sight or makes him blind? Is it not I, the Lord?" (Exodus 4:11). God intricately knows our strengths *and* our flaws. If God were to answer for us that infamous interview question "What are your top three strengths and weaknesses?" he could fill the entire paper. He is sovereign over both our strengths and our weaknesses. He will compensate for our flaws if we wisely seek to do his will.

Conclusion

Who is the best authority on what a person believes? Shouldn't it be the individual person that believes what they believe? How is it, then, that many self-proclaimed Christians don't even know the gospel message; the good news—the significance of Jesus' death and resurrection? Peter instructs us to

---

[4] Garth Jennings, *The Hitchhiker's Guide to the Galaxy*. United States: Touchstone Pictures, 2005.

Faith Saves

"Always be prepared to give an answer to everyone who asks you to give the reason for the hope that you have" (1 Peter 3:15). This is the gospel message. Yet many Christians are dumbfounded when asked for this most basic tenet of their own belief system. There's much to learn from the New Testament, but this is the main point. The gospel message is the most basic and crucial bit of knowledge for a Christian to understand.

We humans often have difficulty remembering everything and miscommunication and misunderstandings abound in daily life. To help combat these issues in the church, creeds have long been used. Creeds state, although in a simplified manner, what we believe. Often referred to as a "statement of faith," churches usually have creeds. If we know our church lists its creed on its website, we may be tempted to send someone there so they can read what we personally believe, even though we've never given any intellectual thought as to whether what the creed states is actually true. Do you know what your church's creed is? If so, have you ever really broken it down and examined the statement in your own mind? Forget about tying each statement to Scripture for the time being; have you even thought about whether you believe it at its face value? Author Eric Metaxas says "We think pointing to these things and saying we assent to them will convince God that we actually *do* assent to what they claim. But God knows better. He isn't interested in what we claim to believe but in what we *actually believe*. And He sees the difference in our lives."[5]

Understand what you believe and don't attempt to outsource your beliefs to anyone else. Neither your parents', nor friends', nor teachers', nor boss', nor church elders'—not even your

---

[5] Eric Metaxas, *Letter to the American Church* (Washington, D.C.: Salem Books, 2022), 64.

pastor's faith can qualify you for salvation. Only your own sincere belief in Jesus can allow his righteousness to replace your sins. Understand the gospel message and fully place your trust and faith in Jesus (reread this chapter if necessary). There is no good thing or any combination of good things you can ever do to earn salvation. Even though it's not any of our good works that save us, we should still expect true, genuine Christians to exhibit good works daily as a result of their obedience to, love for, and appreciation of God.

Comparing us to land, the writer of Hebrews says, "Land that drinks in the rain often falling on it and that produces a crop useful to those for whom it is farmed receives the blessing of God. But land that produces thorns and thistles is worthless and is in danger of being cursed. In the end it will be burned" (Hebrews 6:7-8). Know that there is nothing—no thing or things—you can do to ever be "good" enough to gain salvation. The only thing we can rely on is Jesus; we believe in him and proclaim him as our Lord. Once we experience this true Christian conversion—at that very moment—we are sealed with the Holy Spirit (Ephesians 1:13), "who is a deposit guaranteeing our inheritance" (Ephesians 1:14) as children of God.

Although our salvation in no way relies on any good thing we might do, good works are nonetheless a necessary result of true faith in Christ. Those good works will look different for every individual. No two people will be exactly alike in their opportunities. Education, career path, home address, grocery store choice, likes, dislikes, and talents among other things all play a role in what good works may be performed by an individual. Even something as simple as what car we drive or what shirt we wore today could either spark or snuff out a conversation. There's no universal prescription for good works that will fit all believers, but there are good works available to be done, both large and small, in every believer's life. Our love for and appreciation of Jesus, along with help from the indwelling Holy Spirit, will inspire us to pursue what is good and righteous (although we'll still make plenty of mistakes along the way). Jesus said, "The good man brings good things out of the good stored up in him, and the evil man brings evil things out of the evil stored up in him" (Matthew 12:35). Our works don't save us, but they give us a great view of what's inside.

When encouraging the Corinthians to donate money to their impoverished fellow Christians, Paul warned that "Whoever sows sparingly will also reap sparingly, and whoever sows generously will also reap generously" (2 Corinthians 9:6). Stick with me! This isn't one of those "give me money" moments. This definitely isn't a prosperity gospel message. Paul notably penned (or dictated) the passage about being content in all circumstances, rich and poor (Philippians 4:11-13). He was a strong proponent of giving money to the church (poor Christians, pastors, and other teachers), but all according to one's means. Use your money, time, and gifts to sow generously for God's kingdom. The reward gained will last for eternity. Jesus said to "store up for yourselves treasures in heaven, where moth and rust do not destroy, and where thieves do no break in and steal" (Matthew 6:20). We work hard to build up a 401k that we might use for ten, fifteen, or maybe twenty years, but we often neglect those things that will reap dividends for twenty, times twenty, times twenty, times twenty… times *infinity* years.

Our mortal lives are important and we are expected to be good stewards of all that we're given, which includes our money. If we have a family relying on us, we need to provide for that family and that should extend beyond our death if we have the capability. 401k, disability insurance, and life insurance are valuable financial planning tools, even for—and perhaps *especially* for—Christians. But seek those rewards that are eternal above those that are temporary. Both have their place, but one is clearly weightier. Just because feeding your dog, or doing the laundry, or even rewarding yourself with a special meal after achieving a goal are earthly matters doesn't mean we can or should ignore these things in favor of eternal things. Sometimes making more money now through the sacrifice of taking a demanding job to get out of debt faster is better than taking that lower-paying job that will grant you the time to seek the degree to qualify you for your dream job. Sometimes sacrifice now in terms of money, time, or awkwardness which leads to eternal rewards is better than riches, fame, or comfort in the short term.

Chapter Three

You Are Forgiven

"Leave your ghosts in the past 'cause you know that you can't go back, but you can turn around." – Casting Crowns[1]

"God could never forgive me." "I've done so many things, I'm just beyond forgiveness." "If you just knew all the bad things I've done, you would agree." "There's just no way that God could ever see past my sins." Has someone you love ever brought this type of concern to you? Did you know how to respond? Or perhaps you were the one with the concerns. How did you work through them? Maybe you still *are* the one with these concerns. You may even be too ashamed or too embarrassed or too prideful to talk to anyone about these feelings. Believe it or not, you're not alone. And what's more, having these feelings is not an indicator that you aren't saved.

Feeling saved is undoubtedly a wonderful thing, but *knowing* you're saved is much more important. Similarly, feeling forgiven and being forgiven are two separate things. Both can be true, neither can be true, or one can be true while the other is not. They

---

[1] Casting Crowns, "One Step Away," track 3 on *The Very Next Thing*, Provident Distribution, 2016, compact disc.

don't necessarily coincide with each other. The writer of Psalm 88 understood he was saved. Verse 1 demonstrates his knowledge of that fact. But verses 3 through 18 certainly show that his feelings were not in line with what he knew to be the truth. It can feel like a Friday, but actually be a Wednesday (this is almost never a fun experience). You can forgive your friend for wrecking your car, but they may not feel that you actually forgave them. We cannot rely solely on subjective feelings where objective fact is concerned.

Accept Your Sinful Nature

Believe it or not, feeling that there's no way that God could ever overlook or forgive our sin is correct. Our God is holy and he cannot allow sin to exist in his presence. Think of the vilest sins you've committed and understand that God can't—and won't—let them slide. You are truly unworthy to be called a child of God. But you know what? Even without the presence of any of those most vile sins you thought of, you're still unworthy of bearing God's name. Having only committed one sin of the most insignificant, minute severity in your life completely disqualifies you from any hope of communion with God.

By this standard, no human can ever measure up. And that's the point. Neither Joe Biden nor Donald Trump can measure up. Nor can Gavin Newsom or Ron DeSantis. Ketanji Brown Jackson and Clarence Thomas are also out of the running. None of our recent politicians make the cut. Neither do Abraham Lincoln or George Washington. Martin Luther King, Jr.? No. Mother Teresa? Negative. Pope Francis? Nope. Think of the best human you can; the one with the highest honors, loftiest achievements, largest following, or greatest social impact. Even that person's sin is too great to overcome the distance between themselves and God. If even the best of us are so vastly inferior to God's holy standard, what hope do any of us, the general masses, have for salvation?

Our capacity to attain salvation is actually quite good. However, our *ability* to achieve salvation is absolutely zero. Through the work of Jesus—his death and resurrection—our sins may be forgiven. Jesus, the only perfect human, suffered through the system of this world and paid the penalty for our sins. Jesus' perfection is complete. He had no blemishes. Only a perfect life could atone for our imperfection.

We are, indeed, sinful. We'll also continue sinning as long as we exist on this side of eternity. But once we accept the salvation through the grace God freely extends to us, we are forgiven for all past, present, and future sins. Jesus already paid the price for *all* of our sins. In addition to paying in full for our sins, Jesus also bestows his righteousness upon us. This sounds like impossibly good news to me! This is like allowing someone to pay a bill for you and they in turn decide to give you a valuable gift, just because you let them pay your bill. It's like if we were to go to a grocery store and fill up our cart. When we get to the checkout, the clerk then pays us for having shopped there. Bestowed with forgiveness in hand and the righteous covering of Jesus, we can have confidence in our eternal salvation.

Throughout our lives, we'll continue to add sins to Jesus' punishment, however his grace is sufficient. "Where sin increased, grace increased all the more" (Romans 5:20). There is no out-sinning God's grace. We mustn't be so arrogant as to think that our finite sins are somehow too much for an infinite God to ascertain, comprehend, overcome, or indeed to forgive. Our badness just isn't good enough to beat the grace of God. By no means does this excuse us from living righteously. See chapter 2 for a fuller presentation of the gospel message and why we can't simply accept God's grace, while intentionally continuing to live a sinful lifestyle.

Discipline Because of Love

Have you ever been in trouble? If you're old enough to read this, then I sure hope you have. Discipline is never a fun experience. Discipline is painful physically, mentally, and/or emotionally. Discipline can ruin things in our lives; plans we've carefully made over weeks, months, or even years. Despite the downsides of discipline, any parent that cares about his/her children can attest that discipline is a very important aspect of a child's development. Every child needs to be disciplined when correction is necessary. Discipline should take the form that best suits the situation—the punishment should fit the crime. When it's necessary, the purpose of discipline should always be to correct bad behavior; not to get back at the child for breaking something, or embarrassing us, or being too loud, or whatever other mischief a child might get into. Discipline is meant to give a negative consequence for behaving badly.

Discipline also exists in corporations, athletic teams, and religious organizations. Ask an HR professional and they'll tell you the main goal of discipline is to correct an employee's bad behavior and bring them from low performance in any given area to high performance. Similarly, when an athlete needs correction, their coach steps in to offer discipline. Depending on the infraction, this discipline might be designed to correct a moral deficiency, a training deficiency, or a strategy deficiency. Religious organizations, too, discipline members and leaders as necessary. In the case of the Christian church, this is always meant to bring the individual to repentance and into a lifestyle consistent with Christian belief. None of these—parents, corporations, athletic teams, or religious organizations—discipline their wards as much as they should at times.

Since discipline is never pleasant, why is it so important? Let's use a clear, easy, and common example. The infamous hot stove. Consider two scenarios:

> 1) A mother watches her child reach for the hot stove. The child ignores her command to leave it alone. Not wanting the child to be severely injured, she grabs the child and spanks him. The child cries, having had his feelings hurt and perhaps hit butt stings a bit. Ten minutes later, the child is playing and having fun like nothing ever happened, but he doesn't try to touch the stove again.
>
> 2) A mother watches her child reach for the hot stove. The child ignores her command to leave it alone. Not wanting to hurt the child, she yells louder for him to stop, but he doesn't. The child touches the hot stove and gets a second-degree burn on his hand. Ten minutes later, the child is in an ambulance. He learned not to touch the stove again.

In both scenarios, the child learned the lesson. But which scenario resulted in less harm? And in which scenario did the mother act in the most loving way? Regardless of one's stance on spanking children, anyone being honest would say the mother in the first scenario acted in the more loving manner. The discipline in scenario 1 was limited in scope, yet proportional to the severity of the crime. Touching a hot stove is a potentially catastrophic event. For example, if the child were to spill a pot of 350° oil on his face and body, his life would be changed forever if he even survived the ordeal. "Discipline your son, for in that there is hope; do not be a willing party to his death" (Proverbs 19:18).

It's obvious that discipline can help physically protect children from doing unwise things like touching a hot stove, running into the street, or going places with strangers, but what about other types of discipline? What about discipline for adults? By the time we become adults, we've typically already learned those obvious things we need to avoid to keep ourselves physically safe. But adults tend to struggle in other ways. Employees, athletes, and religious leaders might become lazy or disregard certain rules. Discipline can help to correct adults when something goes wrong with their internal compass. Sometimes discipline can be as simple as the embarrassment of having the behavior acknowledged by another person. Sometimes it might mean a formal write-up, or requiring an additional project to be completed. Or in more extreme cases, it could even mean temporarily or permanently being banned from an organization. With the exception of a permanent ban, all of these forms of discipline are, or at least should be, designed to correct the individual's behavior and bring them back into a good, positive standing with the organization. This type of discipline, then, is an act of love for the offender.

Children need discipline, adults need discipline, Christians need discipline—even Christian adults need discipline. Indeed, those who have our utmost respect as religious leaders still need and undergo discipline from time to time. However, God's discipline can look very different from that done by human hands. "When we are judged by the Lord, we are being disciplined so that we will not be condemned with the world" (1 Corinthians 11:32). Sometimes human discipline is delivered out of anger and it's sometimes even designed to hurt, rather than correct. Abusive parents or corrupt bosses are all too common. Not so with God's discipline. His is always designed and delivered justly and mercifully. God's righteous discipline is always administered out of love for the individual and with the goal of repentance. Here, it's important to make a distinction between discipline and punishment. Punishment is also in God's realm, but this is reserved for those who would not believe. Hell is real and despite his best efforts to the contrary, God will send deserving people there.

Repent

We need forgiveness! An important step toward that end is repentance. We must turn away from our sinful lifestyles and turn toward God. The church is filled with people bearing marred pasts. If the church was perfect, there would be no need for a savior. Peter says we've lived like pagans long enough (1 Peter 4:3). Paul adds, "Neither the sexually immoral nor idolaters nor adulterers nor male prostitutes nor homosexual offenders nor thieves nor the greedy nor drunkards nor slanderers nor swindlers will inherit the kingdom of God. And that is what some of you were" (1 Corinthians 6:9-11). This same Paul, the former murderer, said, "Here is a trustworthy saying that deserves full acceptance: Christ Jesus came into the world to save sinners—of whom I am the worst" (1 Timothy 1:15). Even our greatest heroes are sinful by nature.

When a mob brought an adulterous woman to Jesus, asking whether or not she should be stoned (as the Jewish law instructed), Jesus said the first one to throw a stone should be sinless. When the mob eventually dispersed from the scene, Jesus asked the woman if anyone condemned her. "'No one, sir,' she said. 'Then neither do I condemn you,' Jesus declared. 'Go now and leave your life of sin'" (John 8:11). Here, Jesus is calling the woman to repentance. He didn't celebrate the fact that she was physically spared, instead he immediately turned to her next area of danger. He didn't come to her rescue simply to save her physical body, while forfeiting her soul. He was aiming for the true conversion of this woman. The repentance of this guilty sinner was Jesus' prime concern. Moreover, how Jesus dealt with the mob may have led some of them to repentance as well. They obviously all realized they were sinful too.

Even though he has always known those who would reject him, God still loves them. Predestination is a topic mentioned in the Bible that people like to debate. God did, indeed foreknow everything and still chose to create those he knew wouldn't choose salvation. Since this is the case, some people call God evil. Paul responds to this false notion with some questions of his own. Paul asks, "But who are you, O man, to talk back to God? 'Shall what is formed say to him who formed it, "Why did you make me like this?"' Does not the potter have the right to make out of the same lump of clay some pottery for noble purposes and some for common use?" (Romans 9:20-21). We, in our finite wisdom, have no leg to stand on against God, in his infinite wisdom. We fail to grasp the significance of the difference between anything finite and that which is truly infinite. Infinite wisdom is infinitely wiser than the wisest finite being. Paul continues, "What if God, choosing to show his wrath and make his power known, bore with great patience the objects of his wrath—prepared for destruction?" (Romans 9:22).

Why are we even talking about predestination here? Isn't this section supposed to be about repentance? The subject of predestination is often used as an excuse to not do the right thing; to not even try. A proponent of this type of thinking concludes that if our eternal destination is already determined, then we might as well live as we want now. In other words, we can't change our destiny. This is a deception. Sometimes the worst deceptions contain just enough truth to make us believe the lie. Yes, God knows what will ultimately happen. But just because all of our future actions are already known by God doesn't mean that we're free from bearing the burden of our choices. They're still *our* choices. *We* must make them. God doesn't make them for us. Writing off our own salvation as impossible due to predestination is a self-fulfilling prophecy—we won't gain salvation because we expected to not gain salvation and acted accordingly. This is also a danger with a slightly different direction of thought as well. Assuming we'll gain salvation if we're destined for it, we assume nothing we do can change that course, so we instead live our lives as we want. This will also result in a lack of salvation in the end.

Paul says, "In him we were also chosen, having been predestined according to the plan of him who works out everything in conformity with the purpose of his will" (Ephesians 1:11). Make whatever you want of Paul's words, but know that God chose to make us how we are. For the elect, we're fortunate enough to have a disposition that allowed us to seek God; to open the door as he knocked. For the citizens of this world, the opportunity is still present. God's offer of grace extends to all of humanity. Regardless of his knowledge of our actions or how he formed us, the choice is still ours to make. Repent!

Conclusion

What's done is done. There's no changing the past, no matter how much we might like to do so. Rather than agonizing over our sinful past, or worse, refusing to believe we've committed sins in our past, we must admit to ourselves that we have sinned. Furthermore, we must admit to ourselves that we *still* sin. Sin separates us from our holy God.

A splinter hurts to remove, but brings relief once it's gone. Wait—are we talking about sin or discipline here? Honestly, this analogy works for both. Sin can be painful to remove from our lives. Our sinful nature wants so desperately to hold on to those things that bring temporary gratification, even though we know they're empty pursuits on the grand scale of eternity. Rest assured that our struggle with sin isn't unique to us. A tactic of the devil is to make us feel isolated and that our sin problems are too great for an infinite God. Paul shares a bit of his struggle with sin, "For what I do is not the good I want to do; no, the evil I do not want to do—this I keep on doing" (Romans 7:19).

Until we put on our incorruptible, immortal bodies, we'll continue to have to face our sin problem. The Apostle Paul continues to be a great source of strength for us in this area. Knowing that the apostle with the credentials listed in 2 Corinthians 11:21-12:10 also struggled with sin helps us know that we're not perfect, but God makes us perfect. Our struggle with sin—no matter how grotesque—is not unique. The only difference between the repentant pencil thief and the repentant mass murderer is how much of God's infinite grace is provided upon repentance. Moreover, Jesus died for us before we even made any decision to follow him; while we were still uncovered by the blood of Christ (Romans 5:8).

Even with God's overflowing grace, discipline is still present and is an important aspect of our lives. I love my children, therefore discipline is necessary. If I chose to overlook all of the bad behavior of my children, then I would be unloving. The most loving thing to do is to prepare them for the world to the best of my ability. That includes negative consequences for bad actions. The world won't shield them from negative consequences, so it's my duty to allow them to suffer through consequences at home, while I can still offer a degree of safety from any permanent negative outcomes.

Above all financial success, positions of power, and personal relationships, the character of my child is my prime concern.

You Are Forgiven

Although it wouldn't be ideal, the absolute sacrifice of these things would be a bargain for the price of a good, strong, steadfast character. This nugget of wisdom comes from an imperfect father. God values our character much more than anything we might gain on earth. As God's children, we should expect our perfect Father to discipline us accordingly. The discipline I may administer is imperfect—sometimes it's too harsh; sometimes too lenient. But God's discipline is always just and perfect. We may not understand why we need to endure a specific round of discipline, but God knows why we need it and how we can grow from it. God wants us to be happy. No, we're still not talking about a prosperity gospel. In fact, we should expect hardships, but that doesn't mean God wants us to suffer unjustly. Although we aren't promised worldly success in this life, God does want his children to be happy. However, far more than happiness in this life, God wants to prepare our character for eternity.

Repent! Nothing you've done in life is beyond God's comprehension, foreknowledge, or grace. You can't out-sin the grace of God. God already knows what you've done, so stop putting off asking him for forgiveness! When you fall prey to your own sinful desires and return to your senses, immediately return to God in prayer. Don't let the devil take yet another win by listening to the lie that God doesn't want anything to do with you, or that God won't forgive you, or that it's pointless to repent because you're too weak-willed to keep from sinning again. God wants *everything* to do with you, he has *already* forgiven you, and you *will* sin again. Remember that many of the most potent lies have enough truth to make them believable. If you've already believed and acted upon the gospel message, God's grace has already covered you before you committed any additional sins today, tomorrow, next week, and even in twenty years. You are covered. Repent! Turn back to God, earnestly ask for his forgiveness, thank him for the grace he's already extended to this situation, and seek his help in overcoming your sinful desires in the future.

Find a trusted friend at church that can help hold you accountable. Form a new habit. When you start having the sinful desires with which you most struggle, go outside for a walk, or call your accountability partner, or read the Bible (perhaps a particular chapter or Psalm addresses your issue), or pray, or maybe it's as simple as going into a different room. Above all, don't let the devil use your sinful nature to separate you from God. If you've already had a genuine conversion experience, then you're already blessed with God's abundant grace. Have we covered this enough yet? I know it's difficult to *feel* forgiven sometimes. I know we instead feel like complete failures at times. But our value is derived by God's view, rather than our own. Frankly, and thankfully, our ever-changing viewpoint is irrelevant, and God's unchanging view, plan, purpose, and promise is what truly matters. And you are beloved.

Chapter Four

The Omnis of God

"There is not one square inch in the whole domain of our human existence over which Christ, who is Sovereign, does not cry 'Mine!'" – Abraham Kuyper[1]

Have you ever stopped to consider the sheer magnitude of God's power? We hear the "in the beginning" story and vastly underappreciate the scope of God's work. This being not only exists outside of space and time, but he actually *created* space and time. Everything that science discovers or has discovered was designed by God. We are surrounded by an unimaginable amount of creative design, yet it just seems normal to us. This is the way the world is, so we think nothing of it. There's a familiar saying, "can't see the forest for the trees." This is you and I. We're standing on the outskirts of a cosmologically-sized redwood forest, unable to see past the very first incomprehensibly-enormous trunk.

Dr. Neil DeGrasse Tyson, the famous astrophysicist, astutely noted, "The universe is under no obligation to make sense to

---

[1] Eric Metaxas, *Letter to the American Church* (Washington, D.C.: Salem Books, 2022), 6.

you."[2] Dr. Tyson is absolutely right. The universe is indeed a vast and marvelous thing. There is much about the universe we still don't know and new discoveries crop up like fruit flies in a spotless home. Where do those guys come from, anyway? There's not even anything for them to eat! Dr. Tyson is correct that the universe has no such obligation. Yet we expect something greater, vaster, and more marvelous to be understandable in every way. What obligation does God, the creator of Dr. Tyson's non-obliged universe, have to be understood by humans?

The universe isn't obliged to reveal itself to us and it makes no attempts to do so. Likewise, God isn't obliged to reveal himself to us, however he *does* make the attempt. In fact, he makes the attempt in some very dramatic ways throughout Scripture. The dramas of Moses, Elijah, and the Apostles come to mind. Yet even without any written words, God reveals himself through his creation. "For since the creation of the world God's invisible qualities—his eternal power and divine nature—have been clearly seen, being understood from what has been made, so that men are without excuse" (Romans 1:20).

Some big words are often used to describe God's infinite traits. God is omnipotent, omniscient, and omnipresent. Omni is just a fancy Latin term that means all. These "omnis," then, refer to God's absolute power, absolute knowledge, and absolute presence. This leads us to three facts that will help Christians understand God better. First, God is all-powerful. There is no logical thing that God cannot do. Second, God is all-knowing. There is nothing that God does not know. Third, God has had the same plan of redemption since before the beginning of time. Through his absolute knowledge of the universe and time and all subse-

---

[2] Neil DeGrasse Tyson, *Astrophysics for People in a Hurry* (New York: W. W. Norton & Company, Inc, 2017), 13.

quent events within the universe and time, God set his plan of redemption in motion from the beginning. Before Genesis 1:1, God knew Jesus would be crucified for the sins of humanity.

God is Powerful

Contrary to what many would initially suspect, the most miraculous... miracle... in the Bible is not the resurrection of Jesus, although that resurrection was vitally important. The biggest miracle happened much earlier in time. Actually, it happened right at the very beginning of time. "In the beginning God created the heavens and the earth" (Genesis 1:1). This is how the Christian (and Jewish) Bible begins; with the greatest miracle to have ever miracled. Yet we just gloss right over it without thinking about how truly awesome this event was. What was there before the beginning? Nothing. NOTHING. No thing. No space. No time. We tend to have a hard time imagining nothing because we're surrounded by somethings; and lots of them. Out of the *absolute* nothing, our "spaceless, timeless and immaterial"[3] God spoke everything into existence.

We humans are lucky if our voice can produce an accurate fast-food order from the drive-through. But God had no such doubts about the power of his voice. With nothing but his will and his word, the earth was created with all of its intricate and inter-reliant systems. The amazing diversity of life on earth was imagined, designed, and spoken into being by God, from the simplest lifeform in the plant kingdom to the most complex one in the animal kingdom. And not only plants and animals, but all the elements of nature; hot and cold, rain and snow. God created wind, water, dirt, and rock. He created salt, basil, and cumin. He created wheat, onions, and corn. He created snails, deer, and

---

[3] Frank Turek, "The Universe Had a Beginning," December 29, 2011, https://crossexamined.org/the-universe-had-a-beginning/.

whales. He created magnesium, sodium, and boron. With his word, God created our solar system, the Milky Way, and all other galaxies and cosmic bodies.

Beyond the things we can see, God used his wisdom and power to create the laws of nature to govern his creation. These laws protect the universe's ability to sustain life and bring order to what would otherwise be chaos. Our universe, galaxy, and solar system are finely tuned to support our life on this planet. God created physics and math and these mediums can be used to accurately describe and even predict how the universe is actually structured. Through math, we can determine there should be another element on our periodic table, even if we haven't discovered it yet. We can calculate the ratio of the gravity on Venus to the gravity on the earth. We can even estimate the age of a star or galaxy or even the universe.

Bringing our attention back to our home planet, we observe something as simple as a bee gathering nectar from a flower and don't realize these completely different species—one capable of a degree of thought and the other not—are dependent upon each other. Neither was able to foster the other's development to meet its own needs, yet both exist; completely separate from one another, but nonetheless reliant on each other. Consider a fruit bush. Lacking any awareness of the world around it, somehow it began producing nutritious and tasty fruit that animals like to eat. The seed is protected to survive through the unknown creature's unknown digestive system and is deposited in an unknown rich fertilizer in an unknown new location, ready to grow and repeat the cycle.

Our world is filled with inter-species relationships that scream, "I'm a product of design!" Christians and most atheists agree that life had a beginning. However, when a Christian points out the preponderance of evidence for the design of life, rather than the greater miracle of life spontaneously forming on its own and developing the seemingly-limitless diversity we experience, the atheist would say the Christian is using a "God of the gaps" argument. The Christian says God's direct intervention is the most plausible cause for the universe to have formed out of nothing. The atheist says we just can't definitively say how the universe formed, but it wasn't God. Isn't this an atheism of the gaps argument? The atheist here seems to have at least as much faith as the Christian. The difference is simply in the conclusion. As Christians, we shouldn't write off any evidence the atheist might bring forth simply because their conclusion is there is no Creator. Yet this is precisely what the atheist is doing. They're following their faith blindly, completely ignoring any evidence that might support a conclusion they think is incorrect.

God Knows Everything

The next time you go outside, pluck a blade of grass and take a close look. Take note of everything you can determine about that small piece of a plant. You could cut it up, look at it under a microscope, or even examine its DNA. Once you've exhausted your resources, consider that God knows literally everything about that blade of grass. In intricate detail, God knows every action and process taking place within every cell of that plant in real time. Not only that particular blade of grass, but God is aware of the inner-workings of every cell in every blade of grass in every city, in every country, on every continent, on every planet. In fact, God's knowledge of your blade of grass goes even further than that. God's knowledge of this individual blade of grass that you randomly plucked on a whim has always existed, even thousands of years before it or you did; even preceding the creation of time. On the day you were born, God knew that you would pluck that specific blade of grass at the exact moment you chose to do so.

God's understanding extends to all animal life as well; all animals that we know of as well as all animals we have yet to discover. God knows all animal life that is extinct too, including those species that we'll never discover. God's creation also extends abundantly beyond our capability to explore. "He determines the number of the stars and calls them each by name" (Psalm 147:4). Every planet, every moon, every star, every comet, meteor, black hole, galaxy, every speck of space dust; God created everything in space. Everything in our physical realm was imagined, designed, and willed into existence by God. And he knew every detail of every inch of his creation across all times within creation before time, matter, and space began. "Before the mountains were born or you brought forth the earth and the world, from everlasting to everlasting you are God" (Psalm 90:2).

"The eyes of the Lord are everywhere, keeping watch on the wicked and the good" (Proverbs 15:3). There is no escaping God's presence or knowledge. Right now, in the past, and in the future; God knows all things from all instances of time at all times. There is nothing that was, is, or will be that God has not known from before time began. When Moses asked God for his name, God's reply was "I AM WHO I AM" (Exodus 3:14). God's name "I Am" is a reference to his unchanging nature. In fact, "I AM WHO I AM" can also be translated as "I WILL BE WHAT I WILL BE." If he is unchanging, then that also means his knowledge is unable to change. In other words, God's knowledge is complete. It's impossible for his knowledge to increase. He does know, always has known, and always will know everything there is to know. God has never been surprised by something—he knew literally every event in literally every location in literally the entire history of history would happen before it occurred—literally.

There's an exchange between Jesus and some non-believing Jews. The discussion references Abraham and Jesus said that Abraham was excited for the work Jesus was going to do. The Jews said that since Abraham had died years ago (two thousand or so, in fact), there was no way that Jesus could possibly know anything about him that they didn't already know. Jesus said the famous line, "Before Abraham was born, I am!" (John 8:58). For those of us that are familiar with this passage, we may recall that the crowd attempted to stone Jesus immediately after he said this. Stoning was no less than a means of execution. It was meant not as a correction to one's behavior, but to kill. This was capital punishment. Did this ever seem odd to you? These Jews understood something that we also need to understand. Jesus was attributing the name "I Am" to himself. Jesus was saying that he is God. The Pharisees and other religious leaders who were present certainly wouldn't have missed such a blatant reference to God, given all their study of the Scriptures. Jesus' reference specifically to his unchanging nature was the perfect explanation for how he knew so much about Abraham, who had lived centuries in the past.

Added to his knowledge of 100% of the events to have ever taken place is infinite wisdom. There is no amount of wisdom—human, angelic, or otherwise—that can outsmart God. "For the foolishness of God is wiser than man's wisdom, and the weakness of God is stronger than man's strength" (1 Corinthians 1:25). We can combine any number of our greatest thinkers, leaders, scientists, and philosophers that have ever existed and never come close to even scratching the surface of God's wisdom. We simply can't measure up. It took an incomprehensible amount of wisdom to design all of creation with all of its variety and the microscopic processes that make it all possible. Yet we think we know better than God.

Job was a righteous God-fearing man whom God allowed to be tested by Satan. Job had a really rough time. Everything was taken from him, including his family and his health. The last few chapters of the book of Job are of God putting Job in his place. Before God's lecture, Job listed out all of the good things he had done and why he was a good person that didn't deserve such suffering. God's response to Job is similar to what we might expect from God if he were to answer our complaints directly.

At the end of the book, God asks Job a series of rhetorical questions. The answers are obvious. God begins by saying, "Who is this that darkens my counsel with words without knowledge? Brace yourself like a man; I will question you, and you shall answer me" (Job 38:2-3). If the Creator of the universe says this to you, it doesn't sound like a comfortable position in which to find yourself. God continues, "Where were you when I laid the earth's foundation? Tell me, if you understand. Who marked off its dimensions? Surely you know! Who stretched a measuring line across it?" (Job 38:4-5). Buckle up, Job! God continues driving his point home throughout Job 38-41.

How does Job respond to God's scolding? In the most appropriate way I can imagine. Humility. Job humbled himself before God, realizing that God's ways truly are best and we have no business telling God how things should be. Job said, "You asked, 'Who is this that obscures my counsel without knowledge?' Surely I spoke of things I did not understand, things too wonderful for me to know" (Job 42:3). After God gives his relatively brief summary of things only God can do, Job is in awe. His mind had been opened to the wonder, vastness, and complexity of the world around him. We also live in this amazing world and take it all for granted that everything just works. But only God was there when he designed it all and spoke it into existence. Job ends his response to God, saying "My ears had heard of you but now my eyes have seen you. Therefore I despise myself and repent in dust and ashes" (Job 42:5-6). This is the appropriate attitude to have toward God.

Job said he had heard of God, but has now seen him. This is such an important realization for Job! And we can learn from it. Job knew about God, just like we know about God. We know he created the heavens, and the earth, and animals, and plants, and water, and air, and yada, yada, yada. We "hear" this, but we never "see" it. We know it, but we never allow ourselves to try to comprehend how enormously massive these claims are. We never think about how our brains run on electricity. How can nothing but an electrical signal cause us to feel pain and tickles? How can that signal make us feel happy or sad? How can that signal translate into intricate muscle movements in our mouth and tongue to produce coherent words and sentences that other people can understand—that is, after the electrical signals in their brains allow the vibration of our voice to be translated back into electrical signals. How much intelligence must one possess to come up with a system like this when no such thinking mechanism exists as a reference? This is just one small example of how creative and knowledgeable, and wise is our God. We're surrounded by such complex processes, yet we see them all as mundane, never appreciating the magnitude of thought required to design each minute detail. It took God pointing out several of his feats, but this is what Job came to realize. Job finally saw God's wisdom, majesty, and sovereignty. Of course, there's no guarantee that our experience will be the same as Job, regardless of our response to suffering, however Job's rightful response led to God restoring his community standing, wealth, and family (see chapter 10 for more on eternal justice and being content through suffering).

There isn't anything that can be said or done that can harm or help God. He is infinite and complete. We can't do or say anything to make an infinite being more complete. Nor can we subtract a finite thing from an infinite being to make him less infinite. Everything we have the power to do is finite. If there's nothing that can help God and the Bible is the Word of God, then logically, the Bible doesn't exist to help God in any way. The Bible is written by God through humans for humans.

So, everything God says is for the benefit of us, rather than himself. Likewise, anything we say to God is for our own benefit too. No question, statement, scolding, or praise that we deliver can affect God or increase his understanding. In one instance where God audibly spoke, Jesus explained, "This voice was for your benefit, not mine" (John 12:30). On another occasion, Lazarus had been dead for a few days, but was about to come out of his tomb very much alive. Jesus prayed, "Father, I thank you that you have heard me. I knew that you always hear me, but I said this for the benefit of the people standing here, that they may believe that you sent me" (John 11:41-42). God doesn't need to say things. On the contrary, we need God to say things!

To be completely honest, I wasn't really a big fan of the book of Psalms early in my Christian walk. I saw it simply as a book of Biblical poetry, but I wasn't really a poetry kind of guy. However, I've since found great comfort through Psalms at different points in my life. The book of Psalms is a collection of prayers (or songs), many of which are from high profile people like King David. Some are joyful and exuberant. Some are dark and depressed. "You have taken my companions and loved ones from me; the darkness is my closest friend" (Psalm 88:18). This is how Psalm 88 ends and the first seventeen verses don't offer any more hope than this last verse. The writer of this prayer was clearly severely depressed at this time. Many Psalms have negative things, but turn to positive at the end; not so with Psalm 88. Having gone through depression myself, I can relate to the writer's feelings. The prayer actually does have one positive statement right at the very beginning, saying "O Lord, the God who saves me" (Psalm 88:1). Speaking only from my own experience, this acknowledgement was probably all the praise the writer was able to muster in that moment. This written prayer, despite offering no solutions or hope for the future, was a source of comfort to me in some of my own low moments.

God was able to use the suffering of this writer to ripple forward thousands of years into the future to comfort me through my own suffering (see more on the ripple effect in chapter 10). This, too, is something God knew when he had the writer record this prayer. Psalm 88 was written for us—it was written for me. In fact, every Psalm was written for us. God doesn't need us to know any of these prayers, but we need us to know them. The Psalms are not only filled with comfort for hard times, but they also help us understand and express our gratitude for, awe of, and need for God. God already knows when we're thankful for him or in awe of him or in need of him, but we might be slower to arrive at that conclusion. Sometimes we need to see the struggles or joys of other believers in the Bible or even in our own time to help us understand our own feelings more completely.

Outside of the book of Psalms, we see examples of God seemingly "changing his mind" on different subjects. One such instance is the grounds for the destruction of Sodom and Gomorrah that we discussed in chapter 1. In Genesis 18, God said he was going to destroy Sodom for its wickedness. Knowing his nephew lived there, Abraham was concerned and pleaded with God. Abraham asked if God would spare the city if fifty righteous people were there, then lowered the number, then lowered it again, and kept lowering it until he reached ten. God agreed each time, then went on his way. God already knew the number of righteous people in the city. He also knew Abraham would go through this whole negotiation with him. Why didn't God just cut to the chase and tell Abraham how it really was? God meant for us to see this exchange thousands of years later. It gives us a glimpse into his nature, both for justice and mercy. It helps us to understand that we can bring our requests to God, but also to know that our wants won't always be granted. God's apparent changing of the criteria was solely for our benefit, not for his own. He already knew the outcome before it happened.

Have you ever trained a dog? It can be really hard work. Some dogs are naturally smarter than others and will pick up a lot of the slack for an inexperienced trainer. Others can be difficult even for those with experience. I have an English Mastiff and let me tell you, he is dumb! But he's a good dog. Do an internet search on dog training and you might find some lists of easy-to-train dogs and those that are less so. English Mastiffs are not easy. They don't possess the intelligence of something like a Border Collie or a German Shepherd. They're also quite stubborn. But they do naturally make great companions and excellent family guard dogs. Mushi's not going to let you come into my house when any of my family is home without the okay from someone he trusts. There are gates around my dining room which is Mushi's room. It's a central part of our open-floor-plan home where he can feel like part of the family even if he's stuck in his room.

Even before I got him, one of the things I wanted Mushi to learn was not to go through doors without an okay. He's nervous in public, so sometimes it works and sometimes it doesn't. But it does work pretty much 100% of the time at home with the exception of storms and fireworks. Even with all gates and doors open, Mushi won't cross the line without permission—regardless of the presence of a human. I could leave all doors open and leave the house for hours and Mushi will stay in his room. How do you teach a stubborn, less-than-intelligent dog to obey such a command when no one is around to correct the behavior? Lots and lots and lots and *lots* of repetition. But the repetition alone isn't going to make him obey the command when he knows you're not present. The key is to let him think you're not there, so he breaks the rule and you can make the correction immediately. And you have to do this over and over and over again. When I first got Mushi and was looking up all things dog training, I came across a list of how easy it is to train different breeds according to professional trainers. As I search the Internet today, I'm able to find several similar lists, but not the same article I found years ago. English Mastiffs were at the bottom of the list, requiring roughly 80-100 repetitions until they learn the command. So, probably around 80-100 times, I hid on the kitchen floor until Mushi didn't think I was around anymore. I watched him through the reflection of the stove, all so I could catch him walking through the open gate and correct the behavior.

I'll often find myself disappointed or frustrated with my dog, or even my children nowadays, and wonder, "Why won't he follow my command?" or "Why does he disobey in the same way every time when he knows it leads to a time out *every time?*" I'll realize afterward that God could ask the same questions about me. I knew Mushi would cross the line, yet I allowed him to do so. Mushi thought he knew the entire situation, but only I did. For Mushi's proper development, I allowed him to have a limited knowledge of things. Our relation to God is the same as Mushi's relation to me in this scenario. God knows every way we'll ever mess up. He also knows the ultimate benefit we can attain if we properly learn the lessons after our failures.

God Has a Plan

Sometimes movies are better when we don't know the plan. There's a character that our heroes are following. No one knows the plan but this guide. Just when things look their darkest and all hope is lost—the enemy has discovered our heroes and they seem to be completely outclassed—the plan is revealed and the tide is turned. The heroes overcome the certain defeat they were facing just moments ago, all due to the mystery plan they knew nothing about. The fact that we, as the viewers, didn't know the plan makes it exciting! It keeps us guessing as to what will come next. How will they get out of this predicament? This type of excitement is great for movies, TV, and novels, but it's not what we want for our own real lives. When it counts, we want to know the plan. Often, after they make it past the trouble, our heroes are angry at the guide for not filling them in on the entire plan. We would feel the same way if we were in their shoes. Knowing what to expect is important to us and helps us choose our words and actions to fit well with the plan.

Just like the guide from our fiction stories, God has a plan. Before he spoke his first word of creation, God knew that humanity would fall to sin. He also knew how to fix the problem for us. He knew there was no way we could ever fix it ourselves. He knew that he would have to bear the burden for us or we would remain forever fallen—forever lost. Before there were humans and land animals—before there were birds and fish—before there were stars and moons and planets—before there were plants and continents—before there was an earth—before there was a time that could be called "before"—God had a plan to save us from our own rebellion.

Unlike our fictitious guide, God has revealed to us the major points of his plan. Jesus, God's only begotten Son, came to the world in humility. He took upon himself the disgrace of human flesh, all so that we could torture, ridicule, and murder him. And not just any run-of-the-mill murder; we murdered him with one of the most painful methods the ancient Romans had at their disposal. Even the worst Roman citizens were too good to be crucified. Only non-citizens were allowed to undergo this extreme form of capital punishment. This was God's plan from the beginning.

We see examples throughout the New Testament where Jesus is in submission to the Father, the first person of the Trinity. Because Jesus is the Father's Son, and the brutal torture and murder of the Son was the Father's will, some have called this "cosmic child abuse" as if we can even pretend to know the true depth or reaches of God's plan. This is not child abuse. The Father and the Son are indeed two separate persons, but they are the same God; they share one infinite divine nature. Speaking of Jesus, Paul says, "He is the image of the invisible God, the firstborn over all creation. For by him all things were created: things in heaven and on earth, visible and invisible, whether thrones or powers or rulers or authorities; all things were created by him and for him. He is before all things, and in him all things hold together" (Colossians 1:15-17). Jesus wasn't created. He is the Creator.

Nothing was created apart from Jesus. He was there at the beginning. Jesus is the Word of God. All of creation came about by Jesus' word. He chose to speak the word to create everything, knowing the result even before he did so. In his divine wisdom, he knew the good that would result is much better than any bad that might also come to pass. The Father didn't force the Son to do anything. The Son, also knowing the Father's will, chose to create humanity and accepted what that meant for himself.

God's plan of redemption existed before redemption was necessary. And even at the exact moment time began, God already knew every means that would ever be contrived to thwart his plan. God rightly says, "I make known the end from the beginning, from ancient times, what is still to come. I say: My purpose will stand, and I will do all that I please" (Isaiah 46:10). The parts of his plan that he can reveal to us, he has. There's a lot of prophecy in the Bible; much of which has already come to pass and still some that has yet to occur—although I strongly believe we will soon see the end of this age.

Any government, manager, or leader knows that there are some things that are better left unsaid until the appropriate time. If a nation's people knew absolutely everything about the government's dealings, it would pose a serious national threat. If a manager or leader were to inform their employees about everything discussed at the top levels of their organization, the employees are being set up for potential heartache. "Sorry, I know I said we were planning to give you a bonus this month, but we decided against it." Likewise, in his infinite wisdom, God knows every piece of information that he can't reveal to us in order for his plan to come to fruition or to achieve the maximum result from his plan. See chapter 10 for a related discussion on this subject.

Neither the revealed nor unrevealed parts of God's plan can be thwarted. Gamaliel, a well-respected member of the Sanhedrin, Israel's ancient religious ruling body, understood this well. After Jesus died, rose, and ascended to heaven, the apostles received power from the Holy Spirit. They spoke powerfully in public to spread the gospel message. On one occasion, the apostles were brought before the Sanhedrin and were ordered to stop teaching about Jesus. The apostles' right response began with, "We must obey God rather than men!" (Acts 5:29). After repeating the true accusation that the Sanhedrin killed Jesus, the Messiah, the religious leaders were understandably upset. In fact, they wanted the apostles to be put to death. This is when Gamaliel chimed in with his wisdom. He recounted a couple stories of rebellion that had taken place and fizzled out. Gamaliel advised that if this rebellion was also devised by humans to let it fizzle out as well. "But if it is from God, you will not be able to stop these men; you will only find yourselves fighting against God" (Acts 5:39). Realizing the futility of attempting to undermine the only truly non-underminable force in (and outside of) the universe, the religious leaders let the apostles go, although this was after having them flogged and ordering them not to teach in Jesus' name anymore.

Conclusion

"Jesus Christ is the same yesterday and today and forever" (Hebrews 13:8). God is infinite. He cannot be increased, nor decreased. God doesn't need anything from us. There is nothing we can do to help God or to hurt him. He is all-powerful, all-knowing, and all-present. At all times, in all locations, and in all circumstances, God is complete in power and knowledge.

We've devoted this chapter to expressing the omnipotence, omniscience, and omnipresence of God. Christians often say things like "God can do anything," or they may quote the popular, yet usually-out-of-context passage, "I can do all things through Christ who strengthens me" (Philippians 4:13 NKJV). But is this true? Is there anything he can't do? Well, there actually are things that even God, with all his power, can't do. After all this hype of how powerful God is and how we humans have no possible way to measure up to him, how can this be true? Let's devote a bit of time to that subject here. In fact, many of the things God can't do, we as fallen humans can. The simple truth is God cannot do illogical things. In other words, God can't do things like the supposed Christian-God-destroying question, "Can God create a rock so big he can't lift it?" For one thing, a rock is a finite thing, so its size can't be infinite.

God is rational and logical. He cannot do anything that is contrary to his nature. The writer of Hebrews mentions something God can't do, saying "it is impossible for God to lie" (Hebrews 6:18). Now this is one that even us feeble humans can do. Doesn't that make you feel great? There's actually something you can do that God can't! On the contrary, I'd rather have God's character to not be able to lie or commit any other sin out of the multitude of sinful possibilities before me. Each sin is something we can do that God can't do. God is holy, therefore sin is against his nature, therefore God committing a sin is illogical.

I've never been one to enjoy school. I see the value in education, but I also know that education does not equal intelligence. In fact, some of the most educated people I've met are some of the least intelligent. The opposite is also true. Just because someone doesn't get a college degree doesn't mean they're not more intelligent than someone with a PhD. And with the prevalence of information available through the development of the internet, anyone can become an expert on any number of subjects with no formal study (of course, some good research practices should be followed).

Throughout high school and college, I wasn't a studier. In high school, my goal was to graduate with honors. This meant my cumulative GPA had to be at least 3.5 and I couldn't have any classes with a final grade below C. I was able to reach this goal throughout my four years of high school without truly studying or even completing most of my homework. I was one of the kids frantically working through as many homework questions as possible in the few minutes before class started so I could get some amount of credit. I almost never did any homework outside of school hours. I would pay attention in class and take the knowledge I gained from those classes to the tests without any study time.

There was one test for which I did have to study. I had a D in one of my science classes. If I remember correctly, it was human anatomy. The only assignment left was the final test. I did the math and determined I needed to get 96% on the final in order to bring my grade up to a C to maintain my honors status. I'm sure you can imagine, but I was pretty worried. 96% on a final is a high score and would likely require some focused study time. To make matters worse, I wasn't a studier. It's not a skill that I had developed. Regardless, I still had to try to pull it off. I went home and studied, and studied, and studied. It must have been at least ten full minutes of studying! Just kidding. I probably studied for a few hours, looking through the textbook as well as previous tests, assignments, and handouts. The test time came and I was understandably nervous. Was my study time enough? Did I study the right things? It was time to find out… I aced the exam. Not only did I get every single question right, but there was also a bonus question that I answered correctly. I ended up receiving 102% on my final, surpassing the 96% I needed to save my honors status. It turned out the time I sacrificed to studying was well worth it.

God doesn't need study time. He was able to have received that perfect score, even though he didn't attend the class. Before it even happened, God knew the content of every page of the textbook, every handout, every previous quiz and assignment, and every class lecture, verbatim. My performance on the test was unsure until it was done. God's performance is always a sure thing. His knowledge of all time—past, present, and future—is perfect. He has never been surprised and never will be. Zero times has anything happened in the history of the universe to which God's reaction was "I didn't see that coming."

From the first moment of the universe's existence, God knew where you would be today, right now. He also knew exactly what you would be doing at this very moment. He knew what you would be wearing, every meal you would eat, and every conversation you would have. Down to an atomic, subatomic, quantum, or any other possible levels, God, at the beginning of time, knew each of those particles and how they would interact with each other today. God's knowledge is absolute. There is literally nothing that he doesn't know. Nothing that was, is, or will be escapes God's perfect knowledge. In fact, this leads to another thing that God can't do. Because God's knowledge is complete, he is incapable of learning. That would be illogical. God cannot become more aware of anything because he's already perfectly aware of everything. Nothing is hidden from God; not even your unspoken thoughts; those you've never dared to utter. David poetically says,

> "O Lord, you have searched me and you know me. You know when I sit and when I rise; you perceive my thoughts from afar. You discern my going out and my lying down; you are familiar with all my ways. Before a word is on my tongue you know it completely, O Lord. You hem me in—behind and before; you have laid your hand upon me. Such knowledge is too wonderful for me, too lofty for me to attain" (Psalm 139:1-6).

We all, indeed, pale in comparison to God. In power, knowledge, and holiness, God surpasses us immeasurably. The common comparison of an ant versus a human doesn't even come close to the distance between us and God. Fortunately for us, the Creator, Master, and Sovereign God of the universe chose to create us with the purpose of having a relationship with him.

There is no higher honor than that which is bestowed upon us by the only infinitely powerful being in existence. From the very beginning, God knew all of the evil that would result from his good creation. More importantly, he also knew all of the good that would result from the evil throughout the millennia. God's plan is perfect and he had already taken into account all of the evil the world would have to offer before sin even existed.

God's perfect plan of redemption has never fallen off course, despite humanity's and the devil's best efforts to the contrary. God's plan cannot be shaken. We won't always see every part of God's plan, but we can be confident that his plan will succeed at every turn. After God gave him a prophecy regarding the end times, Daniel was confused. When he asked for clarification, the response he received was, "Go your way, Daniel, because the words are closed up and sealed until the time of the end" (Daniel 12:9).

We aren't meant to know every detail of God's plan. In fact, if every detail was made plain for all, then the plan would likely have to change anyway. No general would give every bit of his strategy to his enemies, or else his plans would be ruined. Likewise, we must learn to accept God's sovereignty over all creation and trust in his perfect knowledge and wisdom. "'I am the Alpha and the Omega,' says the Lord God, 'who is and who was and who is to come, the Almighty'" (Revelation 1:8). God will bring about the perfect outcome in a perfect way. Hope and trust in his perfect power, knowledge, and plan. He can and will do what he says.

"Yours, O Lord, is the greatness and the power and the glory and the majesty and the splendor, for everything in heaven and earth is yours. Yours, O Lord, is the kingdom; you are exalted as head over all" (1 Chronicles 29:11).

Part Two

Cheetos and Cheerios

Chapter Five
Jesus, the Lion

"There's more to being king than getting your way all the time." – Mufasa[1]

Patient, tolerant, abounding in love, forgiving, humble, willing to serve, pacifist; our Lord, Jesus, is a very loving and accepting God. He understands our needs, our wants, and our desires, not only because he's God and through him, all of space, time, and matter was created (John 1:1-3), but also because he forsook his rightful divine place to humble himself with human flesh. He has experienced pain, hunger, sorrow, and anger—he even experienced temptation. Although he overcame the world in all its evil, he still willingly became a part of it. He has firsthand experience with our struggles and knowing this provides us with a great source of comfort. Because he experienced life as a human, we know that Jesus understands the thoughts and emotions surrounding all that tempts us or wears us down. Jesus truly is a gentle and patient Lord.

---

[1] Roger Allers and Rob Minkoff, *The Lion King*. United States: Walt Disney Pictures, 1994.

As we discussed in chapter 2, we're saved through our faith in Jesus. As a result of this faith and the work of Jesus, we can confidently approach God in prayer. He will forgive us when we repent of our sins. Jesus knows that we'll continue to sin as long as we're stuck in our mortal flesh. "For the sinful nature desires what is contrary to the Spirit, and the Spirit what is contrary to the sinful nature" (Galatians 5:17; also see Romans 7:15-25 for Paul's personal struggle). Sin is definitely a problem, however sin may not be our greatest sin when it comes to sin. Are we lost yet? Call this statement (or just me) an oxymoron if you want, but blatant, wanton sin is often better than any level of willful, unrepentant sin.

Grace Abounds

Since the church's inception, there have been those who think sin doesn't matter because the depth of God's love has no limits. Abounding in grace, he is quick to forgive. If we were to think about it, I'm sure we could make a quick mental list of some people we know or even people we see on TV, movies, social media, etc. that seem to believe this false notion. Paul even admits that "where sin increased, grace increased all the more" (Romans 5:20)! So, there is indeed some truth to the sentiment. However, it's still false. For one thing, evil works are evil, but a truly converted Christian will produce good works (see chapter 2 for more information on this point). Additionally, "we died to sin; how can we live in it any longer?" (Romans 6:2).

We see a prime example of the grace of Jesus in John 8:2-11. We briefly discussed this story in chapter 3. The teachers of the law and the Pharisees, always looking to catch Jesus in a trap, brought a woman to Jesus, accusing her of being caught in adultery. Since the Jewish law commanded such adulterers to be stoned to death, they asked Jesus if that's what they should do. Now there are some things wrong with this picture. First of all, these teachers and Pharisees were the Jewish elite. They knew the law and what it required, so there was no need for them to bring the woman to Jesus for his opinion. Additionally, where was the man? The law clearly said that this scenario required both adulterers to be put to death (Leviticus 20:10), another fact of which these teachers would have been well aware.

So, what was Jesus' response? He bent down and started writing in the dirt with his finger. After a while, Jesus said, "If any one of you is without sin, let him be the first to throw a stone at her" (John 8:7), then went right back to writing in the dirt. What, exactly, was Jesus writing? Unfortunately, the Bible doesn't actually reveal this information to us. There's good reason to believe he was writing the ten commandments, or just sins in general. While Jesus was writing, everyone slowly deserted the scene. The older men left first with the younger ones eventually leaving as well. If the theory is correct, it would make a lot of sense as to why the older men fled the area sooner. The older men had more time on earth to study and to gain firsthand experience of breaking plenty of laws. In the end, when Jesus and the woman were left alone, Jesus told her that he did not condemn her. What a gracious gift she had just received! She went from being dragged out by an angry mob into the temple courts, expecting to be killed to having Jesus tell her she would not be condemned. However, the next thing Jesus said to her is perhaps more important. Jesus said, "Go now and leave your life of sin" (John 8:11). Jesus' expectation was for the woman to repent from her sin and presumably to seek salvation.

We have been baptized into Jesus' death to live a new life (Romans 6:3-14). "Therefore do not let sin reign in your mortal body so that you obey its evil desires" (Romans 6:12). Our eternal life begins the moment we put our full faith in Jesus as our Lord and Savior. We are no longer fit to be held captive to sin. So, stop sinning! Once we experience that true conversion, whereby we put 100% of our faith, hope, and trust in Jesus—and we put his desires above our own—we know that our eternal life is not at stake when we do fall prey to our temptation. We are firmly in the hand of the Father and the Son (John 10:28-29). The Holy Spirit within us, by whom we have been baptized, will convict us and lead us to repentance, but our salvation is not at stake. The one caveat here is a major one: Our salvation is not at stake *if we truly have that salvation in the first place* (See chapter 2 for more information on the gospel message of faith and grace. This is literally the most important thing for your personal life in all of eternity, past, present, and future—to infinity!).

Let's talk a bit more about this once saved, always saved concept. It certainly isn't a test for orthodoxy, so feel free to disagree. Belief in or against the idea isn't a salvation issue. In fact, I used to think one's salvation could indeed be lost. After more study and thought (and hopefully increased wisdom!), I've come to believe that salvation cannot be lost. However, this belief demands a great deal of caution. Just as I did prior to my thought change on this subject, I still believe that the once saved, always saved philosophy can be very dangerous without a full understanding. Afterall, if nothing can remove one's salvation, what's to stop him/her from wantonly sinning? This statement, "once saved, always saved," has two parts. We tend to focus on the second "always saved" half, but the first half is just as important! In order to enjoy the always saved blessing, we must be saved in the first place.

We've already mentioned that no one can be plucked from God's hand. There is *no* power that can remove us from God's hand; no earthly or spiritual power. Paul puts it this way, "I am convinced that neither death nor life, neither angels nor demons, neither the present nor the future, nor any powers, neither height nor depth, nor anything else in all creation, will be able to separate us from the love of God that is in Christ Jesus our Lord" (Romans 8:38-39). While I am abundantly aware that I'm overly confident of my abilities on far too many occasions, I'm of the firm belief, and rightly confident, that there's nothing I could ever do to outmatch God's strength, wisdom, love, or will. If nothing can snatch me out of God's hand, that also means my poor decisions can't snatch me out of God's hand. Let's let Jesus' words speak for themselves: "You do not believe because you are not my sheep. My sheep listen to my voice; I know them, and they follow me. I give them eternal life, and they shall never perish; no one can snatch them out of my hand. My Father, who has given them to me, is greater than all; no one can snatch them out of my Father's hand. I and the Father are one" (John 10:26-30). As a side note for those who deny Jesus' divinity, this statement seems to be a pretty strong divine claim.

Lately, it seems every week we can find another prominent Christian, or at least a famous person, that has "deconstructed," left Christianity, and forsaken their faith in Christ. Are these people "always saved?" I don't believe so. And while this may sound harsh to some, the truth is important. What you don't know can in fact hurt you. To use another old saying, the truth often hurts. Just because we don't like to hear or think about something, doesn't make it less true. John actually comes to the same conclusion regarding these "deconstructors," saying "They went out from us, but they did not really belong to us. For if they had belonged to us, they would have remained with us; but their going showed that none of them belonged to us" (1 John 2:19).

A final point we'll consider here for the once saved, always saved belief is one of timing. When we have our true conversion experience, that is the moment we have gained eternal life. Jesus said, "I tell you the truth, whoever hears my word and believes him who sent me has eternal life and will not be condemned; he has crossed over from death to life" (John 5:24). Our bodies will be changed at the resurrection, but our eternal life has already begun. Something that is eternal does not end. If we gain eternal life at the moment we truly place our faith in Jesus and something that is eternal does not end, it would seem that once a person is saved, they are always saved. They have eternal life, which will never end.

You may be wondering of me, "If you believe 'once saved, always saved' is true, but not an essential doctrine, why argue for it here? And if it's Scriptural and true, how can it possibly be dangerous? And if it's dangerous and not essential, why not let some people simply believe that salvation can be lost?" Since this topic is debated among Christians, people may be curious and this is simply some of the fruit of my own study. As Christians, we should be obsessed with truth! We should seek not only to know *that* we believe, but also *why* we believe. You remember Peter's line, "Always be prepared to give an answer to everyone who asks you to give the reason for the hope that you have" (1 Peter 3:15). If Christianity is not true, then "we are to be pitied more than all men" (1 Corinthians 15:19). But let's keep in mind this book isn't intended to explore those answers. There are many good sources for that type of apologetic information. Although it's a bit older at this point (2004), see *I Don't Have Enough Faith to Be an Atheist* by Norman L. Geisler and Frank Turek, for one good example.

As for the danger, let's cut right to the chase. When the day comes that we encounter Jesus in all his majesty, and we must account for the fruits of our lives, we'll tell him all the things we did in his name. "Lord, I went to church most weeks. I donated

Jesus, the Lion

money to the church and other charities as I had means. I was always nice to people. *I'm a good person.*" Jesus' response to many people will be "No man is good. Being good by human standards can never measure up to my Father's glory. You did not seek me or you would have found me. I stood at the door your entire life. If you had only opened that door, I would have given you everything in my kingdom. As it stands, you never knew me. Depart from me, you evildoer!" Of course, this is an adaptation of Jesus' words in Matthew 7:21-23. Many people are deceived into believing they're Christians.

The Bible is clear that spiritual forces are at work in this world and false Christianity is undoubtedly one of Satan's schemes. If we can be lulled into a false sense of security—if we can be made to think we're Christians when we're not—then we pose no threat to the enemy. We're playing right into his hands. In the name of Jesus, we're serving the devil and don't even realize it.

So, the danger of the "once saved, always saved" philosophy lies with the unsaved person. If the unsaved has a false conversion, perhaps simply due to an improper understanding of the gospel message, he or she will not be filled with the Holy Spirit. Without the Spirit's presence, the individual will continue on with life—sometimes sinning, sometimes not—with full assurance that the emotional feeling they had at the time of their false conversion confirms they are heirs of eternal life. Of course, the "salvation can be lost" view also doesn't guarantee a future true conversion, but at least it incentivizes the individual to continue searching and learning. More time seeking God's will would naturally lead to a greater chance of true conversion in the future.

Why even bother making the correction then? In fact, wouldn't we be better off teaching the other doctrine? First and foremost, we want the truly "once saved" piece of the puzzle.

However, the "always saved" piece is a large part of the equation too. It offers great assurance to us when we mess up. And when we do it again. And again. Until we're clothed with incorruption (1 Corinthians 15:53-54), we will continue to fall short of God's perfection. Rather than being fearful that we might die in our sin and be eternally separated from God, we can rejoice in knowing that Christ's sacrifice has made atonement for our sins before we commit them. That forgiveness, while available to all, is only enacted for some. See chapter 2 for more on the gospel message and how to take hold of the free gift of God's grace through faith alone.

Choose Your Master

Slavery is bad! Very few Americans nowadays would disagree with that statement, publicly or privately. Forcibly enslaving another human against their wishes and expecting them to do whatever you ask, often at threat of punishment, is inhumane and downright evil. Modern Americans largely understand this. We're fortunate enough to live in a society that has outlawed slavery, so we don't have to deal directly with those current-day issues. However, the slave trade is indeed alive and well. You may be aware of human trafficking going on in many other parts of the world. It truly is a horrible practice. But did you know that slavery exists in our modern, civilized United States as well? There are many good organizations whose sole mission is to free those people—mostly women, but men as well—held captive by these human traffickers. Having their freedom taken from them, then newly restored, hearing the stories of some of these people can bring forth many different emotions; sadness, anger, disgust, frustration, fear, and anxiety to name a few. Now what if I were to tell you that you are, in fact, a slave? Would you believe me?

Jesus, the Lion

What if I could point to the Biblical case for your slavery? Let's get into it.

Let's start by heading off the likely assumption. We're not just talking about people that haven't truly converted to Christianity. I don't know who might read this book, so I certainly couldn't make an assumption about your salvation! Nevertheless, it is still a Biblically sound accusation. Every human is a slave, and salvation doesn't even play a role in that fact. You're either a slave to sin or you're a slave to righteousness. "Don't you know that when you offer yourselves to someone to obey him as slaves, you are slaves to the one whom you obey—whether you are slaves to sin, which leads to death, or to obedience, which leads to righteousness?" (Romans 6:16). There is no in-between. To make no choice is to choose sin as your master. The great thing about it is we do get to choose our master. One master leads to death and the other to life. I know which one I'd prefer.

Speaking of serving both God and money (an idol), Jesus said "No one can serve two masters. Either he will hate the one and love the other, or he will be devoted to the one and despise the other. You cannot serve both God and Money" (Matthew 6:24). We shouldn't limit Jesus' statement simply to money. In fact, go ahead and replace the word "money" with anything that you put before God in your life. "You cannot serve both God and career," "you cannot serve both God and cars," "you cannot serve both God and clothes." Go for it. Let's make this personal! What is it for you? Is it your appearance? Are you addicted to any drugs? Does your gaming come before God? What about your pornography addiction? You cannot serve any of these masters and still hope to serve God. As Christians, we recognize our position; we used to be slaves to sin. But by the grace of God and through the power of the Holy Spirit within us we have been granted the freedom to serve the master we choose (Romans 6:18). We choose to serve God—to seek his will, and to do good in his name.

Let's be honest here. Some masters are generous and others are more malevolent. Since we must choose a master, what is the reward from each? Paul gives us that answer. "The wages of sin is death, but the gift of God is eternal life in Christ Jesus our Lord" (Romans 6:23). There was no benefit in serving sin—in chasing after death. In fact, we find nothing but shame in how we used to serve our former master (Romans 6:21). "But now that you have been set free from sin and have become slaves to God, the benefit you reap leads to holiness, and the result is eternal life" (Romans 6:22).

The Lion of Judah

500 pounds of fierce, untamed power, a lion's roar can be heard five miles away. This distant thunder would be cause enough for alarm, but coming face-to-face with an angry lion is an even more unfortunate position in which to find oneself. Many Americans probably don't really appreciate the raw power and ferocious presence lions possess. We only see them in zoos, safely behind steel bars. But an encounter with a wild lion with no such barrier in place would carry with it a much more ominous tone. Claws, strong as carbon steel, teeth, a staggering 2.5 inches, standing a whopping four feet tall at the shoulder, this is one terrifying cat. A group of lions is called a pride and he is extremely protective of his pride—his family.

We often hear Jesus referred to as a lamb. And Jesus is indeed the Lamb of God who gave his life to atone for our sins so we could be adopted into God's family. Sheep tend to be docile and non-confrontational. This is the picture Jesus portrayed when the time of his sacrifice came. But there's another animal to which

Jesus, the Lion

Jesus is often compared; one that commands much more fear and respect than a lamb. Jesus is the Lion of Judah. Judah, of course, is one of the twelve tribes of Israel. Jesus was born into the tribe of Judah, so this explains why Judah. But why is he a lion? We're often told of Jesus' love, kindness, and patience, but we don't always hear of his anger, power, and justice. These latter characteristics are just as much a part of Jesus' personality as the softer, former attributes. Jesus tells us his earthly life was not meant to lovingly affirm everyone's misguided sinful natures, but instead was meant to divide us. "Do you think I came to bring peace on earth? No, I tell you, but division" (Luke 12:51). We are being winnowed, separated into wheat and chaff (Matthew 3:12); sheep and goats (Matthew 25:33).

Jesus is a powerful lion who has overcome sin and death. "See, the Lion of the tribe of Judah, the Root of David, has triumphed" (Revelation 5:5). As the Lamb, Jesus went to his death on a cross, bearing the sins of all who would follow him. As the Lion, Jesus rose from the grave, victorious over death. The book of John gives us a glimpse of Jesus' righteous anger. Jesus came to Jerusalem for the Passover and went to the temple. When he arrived, he found it less like the house of God it was meant to be and more like a marketplace. "So he made a whip out of cords, and drove all from the temple area, both sheep and cattle; he scattered the coins of the money changers and overturned their tables" (John 2:15). This was by no means a peaceful event! Can you imagine? A single man clearing the temple area. The temple court could hold several tens of thousands of people, perhaps even multiple hundreds of thousands at times. Since this was around the Passover, where Jerusalem would have seen a large influx of visitors from outside the city, it's reasonable to expect a large gathering around the temple at that time. Jesus experienced anger when God was being used as a means to increase personal standing and as a money-making scheme. Remember that our hearts are not a mystery to Jesus. Do your Christian motivations please him? Are there things he would like to see driven out of your life?

What about now? Has Jesus transcended his righteous fits of anger since he's no longer bound to a mortal body? Nope! I'm not sure there's a better answer than the depiction in Revelation 19:11-16, when Jesus will come back at the end of the age:

"I saw heaven standing open and there before me was a white horse, whose rider is called Faithful and True. With justice he judges and makes war. His eyes are like blazing fire, and on his head are many crowns. He has a name written on him that no one knows but he himself. He is dressed in a robe dipped in blood, and his name is the Word of God. The armies of heaven were following him, riding on white horses and dressed in fine linen, white and clean. Out of his mouth comes a sharp sword with which to strike down the nations. 'He will rule them with an iron scepter.' He treads the winepress of the fury of the wrath of God Almighty. On his robe and on his thigh he has this name written: KING OF KINGS AND LORD OF LORDS."

I don't know about you, but this sounds like it would be absolutely terrifying to Jesus' enemies. Keep in mind that space, matter, and time all came into being due solely to God speaking it into existence. Through the words of Jesus, the universe was created (John 1:1-3). The sharp sword coming out of Jesus' mouth is a reference to the power Jesus, the Word of God, holds. With just a single word, Jesus can overpower the mightiest army. This is the ferocious power Jesus wields.

To go even further, Jesus commands an army greater than any force we have ever seen! Every time I hear Chris Tomlin's song

"Whom Shall I Fear," I think back to an Old Testament event. The chorus has a line, "the God of angel armies is always by my side,"[2] that always reminds me of 2 Kings 15-17. The prophet Elisha was surrounded by an enemy army. *Elijah* (with a "J") is probably more of a household name than Elisha. Elisha was Elijah's disciple and successor; he inherited a double portion of Elijah's spirit (2 Kings 2:9-14). So, what did Elisha do when faced with these overwhelming odds? While everyone around him panicked and asked him for guidance, Elisha remained calm. He prayed. Actually, Elisha's prayer wasn't even to receive God's help. He knew it was unnecessary because God's help had already arrived. Instead, Elisha prayed to open the eyes of his companion, so he could also see. What he saw, I'm sure, was breathtaking. Once God had opened the man's eyes, he saw horses and chariots of fire covering the land; a force much larger and far stronger than the enemy. This is God's army—this is just a small portion of the power that Jesus commands. Even if Jesus, by his wisdom, doesn't just poof his enemies away with a word, his overwhelming army is willing *and able* to get the job done.

    A male lion sleeps most of the time; up to 20 hours per day. Just because he's usually asleep, it would be foolish to think he's not dangerous. Just because he's asleep doesn't mean he's not powerful. Just because he's not actively hunting or driving off the enemies of his family doesn't mean he's not capable or won't take care of the job when the time comes. Just because Jesus is patient doesn't mean he is unable to act. Just because Jesus is loving doesn't mean he is unable to judge justly. Just because Jesus is not defeating his enemies now doesn't mean he won't defeat them at the appointed time.

---

[2] Chris Tomlin, "Whom Shall I Fear," track 3 on *Burning Lights*, sixstepsrecords, Sparrow Records, 2013, compact disc.

Peter reminds us that time is very different in God's eyes than in our own. We mustn't believe that since it seems like a long time, God won't keep his promises. Until the end of the age, people will continue making the choice to follow God. We will continue gaining brothers and sisters in Christ until the moment God knows is best to act. Once that final brother or sister joins the kingdom, God will set the end in motion. Peter goes on to say, "But the day of the Lord will come like a thief. The heavens will disappear with a roar; the elements will be destroyed by fire, and the earth and everything in it will be laid bare" (2 Peter 3:10). Jesus' main goal at this time is to increase the number of humans saved. Since we know of God's infinite love, mercy, and justice, we also know this world, with all the evil that God allows to transpire, must be set up perfectly for God's plan of salvation. But when the appointed time comes, the Lion of Judah will take action. And it will be the most dreadful day for his enemies.

Conclusion

Through Jesus' effort alone, we're offered an immeasurable amount of grace to cover our sins. The more sins we commit, the more grace there is to cover them. We must not abuse Jesus' work on the cross. Those who do "are crucifying the Son of God all over again and subjecting him to public disgrace" (Hebrews 6:6). God's loving, patient, and gracious grace should never be misused by someone who claims to love Jesus. If you were going to participate in a race, you would train and work hard to succeed in that race. Christians must serve God in such a manner as to win the race. At the end of your life, make sure you can look back and say with Paul, "I have fought the good fight, I have finished the race, I have kept the faith. Now there is in store for me the

Jesus, the Lion

crown of righteousness, which the Lord, the righteous Judge, will award to me on that day" (2 Timothy 4:7-8).

Whether we realize it or not, we are serving a master. We can make the deliberate, free-willed choice to serve God or we can choose to serve sin. Even if we don't consciously make either choice, then our choice to serve sin is made. Different masters rule in their own, distinct way and these two are no exception. One master promises happiness, fulfilment, relationships, or money in this life, but results in eternal death. The other master promises tribulation, ostracization, or even martyrdom in this life, but results in eternal life. Most people will take the easy route. They'll choose the master that promises an easier life now (Matthew 7:13-14). As Christians, we shouldn't be surprised when trouble comes. Our old master is always lurking, waiting for our weakest moment to offer us the world—his kingdom. But his kingdom will not last; it is doomed to destruction.

As Christians, we're not promised an easy life. To the contrary, the Bible actually tells us we will face trials. Jesus himself said "In this world you will have trouble. But take heart! I have overcome the world" (John 16:33). All of the Apostles except for John were martyred for their faith. If you're not familiar with the term, "martyred" is a fancy way of saying they were killed for refusing to renounce their faith in Jesus. That is certainly a contrary life outcome to what any prosperity gospel preachers will tell you (see chapter 10 for more on life's hardships and see chapter 2 for a presentation of the Biblical gospel message). When trouble comes, *and it will come*, we can take comfort in the fact that Jesus has overcome the world. There is no power greater than God. Know that Jesus is the Almighty God and no power can stand against his sovereign plan. Know that Jesus is patient and meek like a lamb at times, but just like a lion, our Lion of Judah will take action when the time is right.

Chapter Six

Choosing Your Friends

"You can pick your friends and you can pick your nose, but you can't pick your friend's nose." – A dad somewhere[1]

"He just fell in with the wrong crowd." How many times have we heard a statement similar to this? Perhaps we've even said it on occasion. Sometimes young people choose their friend groups poorly and their behavior suffers for it. They may begin failing classes in which they formerly excelled. They may begin interrupting class and giving the teacher a hard time. Or they may cause trouble at home with their siblings or parents. We intuitively know that friends play a large role in shaping the character of children, teenagers, and even young adults. But to our own demise, we often seem to think that we're completely individual and immune to the leanings of our friends.

Solomon—you remember. The wisest human to have ever existed—said "A righteous man is cautious in friendship, but the way of the wicked leads them astray" (Proverbs 12:26). If Solomon, in all his wisdom, taught that wicked people can lead

---

[1] Dads, *Every Opportunity for a Dad Joke*, Anywhere English is spoken, 1873-present

us down the wrong path, then it's probably a lesson we should learn for our own lives. Notice, Solomon said "man," rather than "child." Solomon doesn't distinguish between ages in this teaching. Yet, despite knowing the right thing to do, this is an area in which Solomon struggled. We find a related command for the Hebrews in Deuteronomy 7, when they were about to possess the land of Israel. The Israelites were instructed not to intermarry with the people in the land. Marrying foreigners was actually an acceptable practice for Jews, however the heart of this particular command was regarding those who worship false gods, "for they will turn your sons away from following [God] to serve other gods, and the Lord's anger will burn against you and will quickly destroy you" (Deuteronomy 7:4).

Solomon came along quite some time after this instruction in Deuteronomy, so he was undoubtedly well aware of the passage. Furthermore, an Israelite king was specifically instructed to "not take many wives, or his heart will be led astray" (Deuteronomy 17:17). Unfortunately, Solomon seems to have ignored both of these warnings altogether. This guy had seven… *hundred* wives and three *hundred* concubines (1 Kings 11:3); one thousand wives altogether. I don't know about you, but I don't even have a thousand people in my life that I interact with on a regular basis, let alone that many wives.

Now, for our purposes, let's just completely ignore the lesson of the one man, one woman Biblical marriage and focus instead on the result of Solomon's marriages. Solomon was not able to remain a steadfast follower of God because of the evil influence of his abundance of wives. Most of his wives likely being marriages to promote political gain, they would have followed religions other than Judaism (this was before Christ, of course). Solomon, wanting to treat his wives appropriately, seems to have spent time with them and sought to understand their viewpoints.

Ultimately Solomon was drawn to these false gods. The result was the loss of God's blessing. Solomon gained enemies and war. Additionally, Solomon's son and successor would end up losing most of the kingdom after his father's death. The sad fate led to the split of the nation into the northern kingdom of Israel and the southern kingdom of Judah. This was all from Solomon not being cautious in choosing his friends (or wives). Their wicked practices led him astray. As the king of Israel, Solomon's choice of friends impacted the entire nation. Unfortunately, the bad company he chose to keep led him down a path toward evil.

By the Company You Keep

Do you remember being in high school when a new student just started? We didn't even have to meet them ourselves to know something about who they were. We were able to draw some conclusions about the person's personality, likes, and values, simply by seeing the people they chose to hang out with. We logically know there is much more to a person than with whom they choose to spend time, but since our brains are built to detect patterns, it really is hard to view the person with a completely blank slate if we know the group they chose as friends. The same is true of how others view us. We're not judged solely by our own actions. Rather, we're judged in light of our associates—our friends.

As ambassadors for Christ (Ephesians 6:20), our image matters; at least to the extent that we can control it. Peter alludes to our public image when he instructs us to "live such good lives among the pagans that, though they accuse you of doing wrong, they may see your good deeds and glorify God on the day he visits us" (1 Peter 2:12). The effectiveness of our witness heavily relies upon how we're perceived by those we're trying to reach. We, of course, have control over our own actions and words, which command a great deal of influence over how others perceive us. Unfortunately, just like most things in life, we aren't in control of absolutely everything. Someone may not like how we look, our facial expressions, our hand gestures, or the shirt we decided to wear today. Perhaps they simply weren't listening to the entire thing we said that was perfectly innocent, but the part they did hear seemed really bad out of the proper context of the entire conversation.

We can't control every variable and we certainly can't control the thoughts and actions—and likes and dislikes, and current mood, and current stressors—of others. People will draw their conclusion apart from our desire for that conclusion to be positive. To mitigate being perceived in a negative light, we often take precautions. We take a shower, brush our teeth, fix our hair, put on makeup, and wear clean clothes so people will perceive us as being someone that cares about hygiene. We select our clothing to ensure we're viewed how we want to be viewed—relaxed, put together, trendy, and so on. When around people with whom we're less familiar, we choose our words more carefully than we do around close friends and family. We naturally understand that our power to control the perception of others is limited, yet we make use of that power as necessary to aid us in being perceived positively.

It may be more obvious in children and teens, but adults have cliques too. Just like their younger counterparts, adults tend to gravitate toward certain types of people, based on their own personal interests. Furthermore, even as adults, we tend to make some judgments about people based on their choice of friends. It would be foolish not to recognize the same is true of the world's perception of us! The company we keep helps inform the world what we're all about. They draw conclusions about what we like and dislike, what hobbies we have, what values we hold, what political party we support, and the list goes on, and on, and on to obscurity. People can draw some very outlandish conclusions from very little data and one's friend group is a rich set of data.

Paul cautions that we "must not associate with anyone who calls himself a brother but is sexually immoral or greedy, an idolater or a slanderer, a drunkard or a swindler. With such a man do not even eat" (1 Corinthians 5:11). Don't even associate with them! Keep your distance. However, Paul gives one major caveat, by specifying the instruction is not intended to mean "the people of this world who are immoral," otherwise, we "would have to leave this world" (1 Corinthians 5:10). Paul's instruction is not meant to pull us away from our task of making disciples of all nations (Matthew 28:19). Rather, the instruction is meant to provide clarity on how to deal with those who claim to follow Christ, but clearly don't live as if they have been renewed by the Holy Spirit.

There were a lot of false teachers in Paul's day and much of the New Testament points out their flaws. Unfortunately, there are *still* a lot of false teachers in our day. Especially with the advancement of technology and the internet, in particular, it's now easier than ever to propagate false gospel messages. Ideas can round the world in a single day. We hear daily that there's a new "viral video." In Paul's time, it wasn't possible to assert your idea and have millions of people see it within hours. Technology truly is a remarkable and terrifyingly powerful thing. Even though the battlefield may look different, the advice is still sound. Don't let yourself be lumped in with a false gospel. John says, "If anyone comes to you and does not bring this teaching, do not take him into your house or welcome him. Anyone who welcomes him shares in his wicked work" (2 John 10-11). John was specifically speaking of those "who do not acknowledge Jesus Christ as coming in the flesh" (2 John 7), a false teaching making the rounds at that time. But John's message also applies in any time period to any false teachers, those who spread a false gospel message and/or live unrepentant in their sin.

Keep It Positive

Have you ever had a friend whose presence just brought negativity? Maybe something in his life is always unfair and beyond his control. Or maybe she talks about everyone behind their backs and some of your other friends have even shared some of her digs against you when you weren't around. Maybe your friend is more overt with her criticisms, even making derogatory comments about you when you're together. Or perhaps your friend is completely self-centered, thinking only of his own interests, while completely ignoring the needs and wants of everyone else. He may expect you to drop everything when he wants to make plans that you don't particularly like, but he'll never return that favor to you unless it's for something he likes. He might even insert himself into every conversation with a story that tops the one that was just told. His story may have some elements of truth, but it's likely exaggerated. The truth is irrelevant to him as long as he wins. Relationships with friends like these often do more harm than good.

How do friends like this make us feel? Is there value in the friendship? Surely there's something good there, but is it overall a beneficial relationship for both parties? Friendship, like any relationship, is a two-way street. There should be a mix of negative and positive things. Yes, negative aspects *should* happen in a healthy relationship. Friends are humans and this life isn't perfect. Therefore, friends will have negative events in their lives. If the friendship is close enough, the parties will share some of these things with each other. Having someone share a negative experience with you, especially one in which you have no control, is never pleasant. It, in itself, is a negative experience for you, the listener. But this is a healthy part of any close relationship. People sometimes need someone with whom to talk out their problems, sometimes receiving good advice, sometimes receiving encouragement, or sometimes just not feeling alone.

We should expect and accept some negativity in our friendships. Our friends, just like us, go through positive and negative seasons in life. However, consistent, excessive negativity may be cause for concern. If it seems our friend only sees the negative in everything, perhaps even oblivious to the self-inflicted chaos they create in their own life, the symbiotic nature of the relationship doesn't exist. Our two-way street has become a one-way street. If we're constantly around negativity, our outlook will be more negative. If we trade that negative atmosphere for positivity, our outlook will be more positive. This is a truth to which anyone who's managed enough people over enough time will attest.

I've managed people over ten years in my professional career. In that time, I've had hundreds of individual employees, managing just under forty at one time. I've experienced many different personalities and how they interact with the other employees and I. It is absolutely fascinating how the job—its duties, responsibilities, and expectations—can stay the same, but the atmosphere varies wildly depending upon the personalities of the individual employees. Through my experience as a manager, I've learned the absolute most important role for one who manages people is hiring. Unless you require a specific set of skills upon hire, the personality of the candidate is far more important than any past experience or education. When I interview someone, I have two main questions in my mind. Question one: Can this person perform the job adequately? Question two: How will this person fit in with my team?

Throughout my management career, I've seen times of high staff engagement and times of low engagement. My personality and expectations likely haven't changed between these times. Rather, the employees have changed; not the employee's personalities, but the actual employees are completely different individuals. I don't say this to remove any blame from me for the low times. On the contrary, one could turn this around and say that the positive times aren't my doing either. Regardless, I believe the manager's personality is very important, since he/she is also a part of the same team. However, the manager simply needs to be adequate. An adequate manager with excellent employees will likely run an excellent team. Hiring is key.

So, what is it about certain individuals that brings the team morale down? There are a number of ways one bad apple can spoil the bunch. There are the more obvious ways of being lazy or even just a sincere lack of competence. Although perhaps what I see more commonly is a personality flaw; constant negativity, inconsideration, or the ability to create drama at every turn, for example. I hired one person to be a work partner for a really good, tenured employee. The new employee worked out great for a while, then the bad traits surfaced. The bad apple was married, but began having an affair with one or more people from other departments, which brought in the family drama, the spouse even showing up to the parking lot. The employee was always out of money, so coworkers helped buy lunch at times. One time, a coworker accidentally sent the employee thousands of dollars through one of those payment apps, rather than the intended lunch money. Unfortunately, a few extra zeroes were added. Instead of immediately giving the money back, the employee spent it. Eventually the money was returned, but it was paid back in increments over several weeks.

Perhaps the most devastating thing to the department as a whole was the employee's attitude throughout their time with us. The normally good, positive, tenured employee that worked closely with the offender was subjected to constant negativity and complaining about the department's leadership. The good employee, being worn down with the same message day after day, began mimicking the same complaints! Fortunately, our offender decided to transfer to do us the favor of accepting a new job, so the problem removed itself. After the transfer, our good employee's mood and disposition toward leadership increased dramatically. There was no change other than losing the bad apple. Sometimes losing an employee, which often results in more work for the remaining employees, brings about increased positivity for those that no longer have to endure such a negative atmosphere every day.

You're Average

You're average! Well, at least you're *an* average. I don't remember who said it, but probably twenty-or-so years ago, I heard something that stuck with me. You are the average of the ten people closest to you. We can clearly see some truth to this statement in our own lives. Many of our habits are learned from friends and family. As much as many of us might hate to admit it, our parents massively Influence who we turn out to become (see, for example, Proverbs 22:6). Our friends also play a large role in the development of our personality and characteristics, especially—but not only—in childhood. The language we tend to use in conversation and our mannerisms; even our beliefs and motivations are to a large degree gained from those around us.

Any of these can be positive or negative traits. There are some other not-so-obvious traits that are heavily influenced by our close relationships. Peace, patience, and kindness, for example, are perhaps a bit more difficult to identify than the previous characteristics.

It's widely accepted that some negative patterns of behavior run in families. Some will get into the argument of nature versus nurture. Genetics certainly predispose us to certain things, but the behavior is still learned, so let's just leave the genetic component out of our discussion for now. Alcoholism is a prime example. Often hiding the negative habit, a child may be oblivious that their parent is an alcoholic. Never having seen the behavior, the child doesn't learn it. Of course, this doesn't mean the child *can't* become an alcoholic, but the chances are drastically reduced without the nurture part of the equation.

How about this one for an example of learned behavior? Domestic violence. If a parent is abusive to his/her child or spouse, the child is much more likely to be abusive to his/her spouse and children. Someone might say they have a gene that makes them more aggressive, but it's still the learned behavior that taught them it was normal or okay. These abused children are actually more likely than the average child to also go another route; they may seek out partners that have those same abusive qualities and become victims all over again; some even repeating this mistake across several different partners. This choice of partners is a learned behavior; there isn't a victim gene, although there may be genes tied to attributes that would make one more susceptible to this cycle. Regardless, the behavior is learned from the people closest to us; parents, in this case.

Of course, your "association average" doesn't just apply to negative traits. So, we should seek out and befriend those who would bring our average up! Just one individual can have a profound impact on a person's life. Going with this average idea, let's say your ten friends are each a 10 on a scale of 100 (if we could even quantify a person). Averaged together, that would make you a 10 out of 100. If you were to replace just one of those with a 100, then your average almost doubles to 19 out of 100. Replace one more with another 100 and you're now a 28.

If you're the average of the ten people closest to you, seek to fill those ten relationship slots with people you want to emulate. People who excel in a career you're pursuing, those who reach high academic achievements, parents who spend time teaching their children outside of school, rather than putting all of that burden on the public school system, people that are good with financial matters and invest their money wisely, individuals who show great discipline in order to achieve personal goals, and, of course most importantly, those who excel in righteousness, who love justice and mercy, and are humble in their walk with God (Micah 6:8); these are some of the types of people that would make great additions to your top ten. Imagine if you were to assemble such a list and became the average of these individuals.

Solomon has more to say on the subject of choosing friends wisely. "As iron sharpens iron, so one man sharpens another" (Proverbs 27:17). This verse is used a lot and for good reason. It calls us into fellowship and reasoning with other people. In any form of debate, whether formal or just friendly conversation, ideas can be challenged. When we allow our ideas to be challenged in good faith—good faith from both parties—it provides us with an opportunity to either deepen our understanding of our own beliefs or to discover that our belief was flawed. Our God is the God of reason (just look around at the natural order, rather than chaos, of the universe). "'Come now, let us reason together,' says the Lord" (Isaiah 1:18).

Contrary to what some might believe, questioning God is actually good as long as it's done in a way that's honestly seeking truth. Since Christianity is true, an *honest* seeker will find it to be truth. God will make sure of that. The book of Habakkuk comes to mind as an example of a questioning dialogue with God. We may not always understand why things are the way they are, but we can always be confident that God uses evil for good (Romans 8:28; see chapter 10 for more on this subject). Seek friends that will keep you learning. Learn why you believe what you believe. Believing something doesn't make it true, so learn why the belief is true.

Paul says "Do not be misled: 'Bad company corrupts good character'" (1 Corinthians 15:33). Heed Paul's warning. Do not be misled! Your character is corruptible. We aren't the stand-alone fortresses of individuality that we often feel we are. To some degree, we're truly the average of that with which we choose to surround ourselves. "Do not make friends with a hot-tempered man, do not associate with one easily angered, or you may learn his ways and get yourself ensnared" (Proverbs 22:24-25). Do you have an anger issue? Fill a slot or two with people that control their anger in a productive manner. Do you struggle with impatience or impulsive shopping? Give a spot to someone that's calm in all circumstances or someone that strictly follows a budget. Seek friends that have the qualities you want to cultivate in yourself. More importantly, seek friends that have the qualities that God wants you to cultivate in yourself.

Conclusion

We must be careful with whom we choose to associate. Not only for the protection of our own values, but also for the validity of our witness. Jesus spent time with the lowest people in society.

Choosing Your Friends

In order to fulfill our task of making disciples throughout the world, we obviously can't isolate ourselves from those people either. The association issue is not to avoid those that desperately need to hear the gospel message. Rather, we should avoid befriending those who claim to be Christians, but live unrepentant sinful lifestyles. Much more importantly, we must avoid aiding in the propagation of a false gospel message. Paul cautions, "Do not be yoked together with unbelievers. For what do righteousness and wickedness have in common? Or what fellowship can light have with darkness?" (2 Corinthians 6:14). The world will judge us by the company we keep and our authority and trustworthiness will wax or wane in accordance with that judgment.

"A cheerful heart is good medicine, but a crushed spirit dries up the bones" (Proverbs 17:22). Seek those as friends that will be good medicine, rather than those that will siphon your life away. If your mental state withers away due to constant negativity, you won't have any medicine left to share with those who need *your* cheerful heart. Choose friendships that are mutually beneficial, rather than those that just go one way; those that stifle all positivity in the atmosphere.

You are the average of those to whom you're closest. Friends and family can pass on their negative attitudes, habits, and beliefs to you. Beware of what you're consciously or unconsciously learning from those around you. Paul says, "let us purify ourselves from everything that contaminates body and spirit, perfecting holiness out of reverence for God" (2 Corinthians 7:1). In order to follow Paul's advice, we of course need to do some serious introspection of our own lives. But we also need to take a look at the people we keep close.

Surround yourself with those that demonstrate the fruit of the Spirit. "The fruit of the Spirit is love, joy, peace, patience, kindness, goodness, faithfulness, gentleness and self-control" (Galatians 5:22-23). Also, seek wise friends that will help you refine and solidify your beliefs—why you believe what you believe. "He who walks with the wise grows wise, but a companion of fools suffers harm" (Proverbs 13:20). In one of his prayers, David said, "My eyes will be on the faithful in the land, that they may dwell with me; he whose walk is blameless will minister to me. No one who practices deceit will dwell in my house; no one who speaks falsely will stand in my presence" (Psalm 101:6-7). Resolve to take David's approach to friendship.

Choose friendships that will lead you to life. As a result, you will become one such friend to others. Being viewed more highly by the world, you will have a greater witnessing platform. Being surrounded by positive thinkers, you will be better able to be content in all circumstances. Being surrounded by more 100s than 10s, you'll be closer to every meaningful goal you set for yourself. You'll become a friend that the world has no basis to judge, you'll bring a net gain of positivity to your friends' lives, and you'll increase the "association average" of those you care about most.

Chapter Seven

Judge Yourself

*"The choices we make are ultimately our own responsibility." –
Eleanor Roosevelt[1]*

"Don't judge me!" "Who are you to judge?!" "It's not my place to judge." We hear these phrases regularly. Perhaps we even use them ourselves. But is it true that we shouldn't judge? Nowadays, we learn how we should look, act, and think through Facebook, Twitter, and TikTok. What happens when we encounter a discrepancy in what we learn through the culture and our Christian worldview? Do we even notice when there is a discrepancy?

Peter says one who follows Christ (that would be a Christian) is done with sin. He goes on to say "he does not live the rest of his earthly life for evil human desires, but rather for the will of God. For you have spent enough time in the past doing what pagans choose to do—living in debauchery, lust, drunkenness, orgies, carousing and detestable idolatry" (1 Peter 4:2-3). If we are to recognize these sins in our lives, it would naturally take

---

[1] Eleanor Roosevelt, *You Learn by Living* (New York: HarperCollins Publishers, 1960), xii.

some amount of introspection. For example, we might be married, yet look at every attractive man or woman with lust. No big deal. Everyone does it, right? Has anyone ever asked you "If everyone was jumping off a bridge, would you do it too?" I know my grandmother's asked that question of me countless times. Regardless of how widespread the action may be, Jesus says this is adultery of the heart (Matthew 5:28). It is most definitely not an easy task and we should expect failure on many occasions, but we must try to remove sin from our lives. We must look into our own words, thoughts, and actions for all traces of sin. Once found, we must take steps to overcome. Some sins will be easier to deal with than others.

You're a Sinner

Can we stop for a minute? I just want to make absolutely sure you know you're a no-good, low-down, dirty, rotten sinner. And so am I! In Romans 3:10-18, Paul reminds us that part of the human condition includes having a heart bent toward evil, even making (or repeating) the claim "There is no one righteous, not even one" (Romans 3:10). John adds "If we claim to be without sin, we deceive ourselves and the truth is not in us" (1 John 1:8), and "If we claim we have not sinned, we make him out to be a liar and his word has no place in our lives" (1 John 1:10).

Still not convinced of your evilness? "There is a way that seems right to a man, but in the end it leads to death" (Proverbs 14:12). Don't be deceived. Perhaps even more importantly, don't deceive yourself! The human mind is a remarkable thing. It protects itself in many different ways. Sometimes it's used to devise a plan of physical protection. More often in our modern culture, it seeks to protect us socially and emotionally. Being wrong, our conscious and subconscious mind reasons, could lead to social ostracization or perhaps just being viewed in a less flattering light. Our minds, sometimes even unknown to us, will develop lies, or bend the truth, or dismiss evidence contrary to our beliefs. There's a term in the psychology world called confirmation bias. A bias, of course, is an idea we typically bring to a situation before we review any evidence of the current situation. Biases are normal, natural, and (within reason) even good! You use your personal experience to create biases for your everyday life, many of which have kept you alive until today. Confirmation bias, then, is when we come to a situation with our preconceived idea, but only seek evidence that proves our idea correct. You could make the argument that it's a defense mechanism designed to protect our pride. When you examine yourself, be determined to let go of that pride and judge yourself honestly. Afterall, God sees your sin regardless of your acknowledgement of that sin. "The lamp of the Lord searches the spirit of a man; it searches out his inmost being" (Proverbs 20:27). Don't be like the confirmation-biased adulteress of Proverbs 5:3-6. "Her paths are crooked, but she knows it not" (Proverbs 5:6). She willfully participates in an outward act such as adultery, but doesn't even realize she's sinning. You have sin; you may just need to be willing to allow your pride to be hurt. Look for the evidence that would disprove your preconceptions. Although he wasn't speaking directly to us, it's still true of us when God says "For I know how many are your offenses and how great your sins" (Amos 5:12).

No matter how good you are, you are failing miserably in comparison to God's standard. Nonetheless, different sins most definitely have differing levels of severity, differing outcomes, and differing punishments. In Luke 12:47-48, Jesus gives us a glimpse of different outcomes even for the same sins. To paraphrase, the discipline is more severe for someone who does wrong, while knowing it's wrong than for the person that does the same wrong without knowing it's wrong. Another way to say this is details are important. Jesus cares deeply for the context of the sin. Punishment (and reward: see Matthew 25:14-30, for example) will be given fairly, but not equally.

Say you're dealing with a friend who's struggling with homosexual tendencies. Often Christians are seen as intolerant and unloving when we point out that homosexuality is a sin. On the contrary, the most loving thing a Christian can do is inform the uninformed that what they're doing is sin, whether it's homosexuality or something else. Sin has eternal consequences. Your child might want to eat that colorful poison or touch that hot stove. Would it be unloving for the parent to stop the child and tell them it's dangerous? Of course, the most caring thing to do is to intervene. Where it seems we Christians may be able to improve is the approach. We need to keep the person's eternal destination in mind, but we also must keep their own free will in mind.

Here's an illustration that makes a lot of good sense in my own brain. Your homosexual friend is certainly sinning if he/she is acting upon his/her sinful desires. We, as Christians, should point out the sinfulness of these actions. Not that I think we should *have* to defend our view on sin, but I think it is a wise thing to do in light of our culture today; tell your friend you believe their actions are sinning against God. But also remind them that all people are sinners (is this starting to sound like the gospel?). If God decided to erase all sin, there would literally be no one left. There are different severities of sin, however that doesn't excuse lesser sin.

Now for the illustration. On a scale of 1 to 100, how far away from God's moral standard is homosexual sin? Think you know the answer? In our own minds, we like to rank sins and say "I may do this, but at least I don't do that." But what's the answer?

It's a trick question! Homosexual sin is infinitely away from our infinite God's moral standard. What about adultery? Infinite. Theft? Infinite. Lying? Infinite. When you lied to your spouse about how they looked in that pair of jeans; even that harmless lie was infinitely away from God's moral standard. The issue with your friend isn't their homosexual tendencies; it's their tendency to sin. And that tendency is the same for you and I. This is precisely why we need a savior. The point of all this is that God is the ultimate judge. We are expected to lovingly inform, but it is up to each individual to do right or to do wrong.

God's instruction to the prophet Ezekiel is helpful: "When I say to a wicked man, 'You will surely die,' and you do not warn him or speak out to dissuade him from his evil ways in order to save his life, that wicked man will die for his sin, and I will hold you accountable for his blood. But if you do warn the wicked man and he does not turn from his wickedness or from his evil ways, he will die for his sin; but you will have saved yourself" (Ezekiel 3:18-19). Taking this into account, we should enter sin-revealing conversations with the hope of leading the person to repentance, but knowing it won't necessarily happen in that moment. Of course, if a sin puts someone in physical danger, we must take actions to protect that person, whether it's self-inflicted or aimed at another party. Putting all other issues aside, if a sinful action were to get someone killed, there can be no further conversations to lead to repentance. So, if it's God's will, our plan should be to plant the seed, knowing it may be someone else that waters it, and it will be God that will make it grow (flashback to the introduction of this book).

Expected to Judge

Doesn't the Bible teach us not to judge? Wasn't Jesus all about love? There's no way Jesus would have judged people. Unfortunately, these beliefs are prevalent in our culture and even within the church. On the contrary, the Bible actually instructs us to judge. In fact, sometimes the most loving thing to do for a person is to judge them! Jesus was a prolific judger. He called out sinners left and right.

Jesus is indeed loving, but love doesn't require acceptance of bad beliefs or behavior. Is a teacher unloving when he corrects a student's false, but genuine belief that two plus two doesn't equal four? Is a father unloving when he disciplines his child for running into a busy street without looking? Is an employer unloving when she administers corrective action to an employee that's spending most of every work day browsing social media? Obviously, the teacher is demonstrating more love by correcting the student's genuine belief. If the teacher affirms the false belief that two plus two doesn't equal four, the student will continue his education journey with a seriously flawed understanding of basic mathematics. The father, too, is acting in the most loving way by using discipline to reinforce the notion that the child shouldn't recklessly run into a dangerous area.

Perhaps less obvious is the employer/employee situation. But even with this situation, the employer is acting in the most loving manner. If she doesn't correct the lazy employee's behavior, the morale and productivity of her entire team will suffer. So, disciplining the offender is the most loving thing she can do on behalf of her other team members. But the discipline is also likely the most loving thing she can do for the employee. Especially if the employee is young and has a long work life ahead of him, correcting his behavior in the workplace early will help him adapt to the demands of working for someone other than himself. If he

Judge Yourself

learns the lesson well, it will enable him to reach far loftier heights throughout his career.

Jesus; our dear, sweet, abundantly-loving Jesus. The majority of people have a warped view of Jesus. Jesus is indeed the Lamb that was slain for our sakes—to pay for our sins. Jesus does indeed love each of us dearly. Jesus loves us as both a father and a brother. Jesus knowingly went to his death—the grueling, humiliating, torturous death on a cross—out of his great love for us. It was his choice. Overwhelming love is certainly a characteristic of Jesus. However, the part we forget is that Jesus is also the Lion; the one who has overcome the enemy; the one who leads the army of heaven; the only one worthy to open the scroll that will set all things right (Revelation 5:5). Jesus is a mighty warrior. No army is more powerful. No enemy is more zealous for their cause. No leader is more cunning. No force on earth or in heaven can compete with Jesus in his divine glory.

Jesus was not a pacifist. He forcibly removed the people that turned the temple courts into a marketplace (Matthew 21:12). In Matthew 23, Jesus delivers a scathing lecture to the religious leaders, even saying, "You snakes! You brood of vipers! How will you escape being condemned to hell? (Matthew 23:33). These aren't the words of someone that doesn't judge others. "Jesus doesn't judge" is a deception of the enemy. Unfortunately, this lie is rampant, emboldening people to live as they want; to be their own god—their own idol.

The Jesus that "doesn't judge" likely comes from a verse handled out of the proper context. "Do not judge, or you too will be judged (Matthew 7:1). Now this verse sounds pretty straightforward, but this isn't the end of the point Jesus was making. Jesus goes on to say "Why do you look at the speck of sawdust in your brother's eye and pay no attention to the plank in own eye? (Matthew 7:3). He finishes his point saying, "You hypocrite, first take the plank out of your own eye, and then you will see clearly to remove the speck from your brother's eye" (Matthew 7:5). Jesus' purpose in this section wasn't to tell us not to judge. On the contrary, Jesus was telling us that *when* we judge, we should first look at ourselves to determine if we "practice what we preach." Jesus says we should examine ourselves and remove our blatant sins before we judge our brothers for their same or lesser sins.

An important note from this section of Scripture is the statement with which Jesus immediately follows his instruction. He says, "Do not give dogs what is sacred; do not throw your pearls to pigs. If you do, they may trample them under their feet, and then turn and tear you to pieces" (Matthew 7:6). So, Jesus' instruction here is to judge those within the church, but be wary of those outside who will refuse to listen. Step one: Examine yourself and remove your own planks. Step two: Examine your brothers and sisters in Christ and gently help them to remove their specks. Step three: Use all the wisdom, knowledge, and discernment you can muster to know when and how to address those who will listen versus those who will not. Jesus generally doesn't want us to waste our time on fruitless endeavors that will only end in frustration at best, or verbal, financial, or physical attacks at worst.

Outreach to unbelievers is certainly an important function of the church. However, in my opinion, the most dangerous thing the church is facing today is a lackluster Christianity. I see the church today as "having a form of godliness but denying its power" (2 Timothy 3:5). If Christianity is true, then there is nothing in all of existence that is more important to you as an individual. If Christianity is false, then it's of no consequence whatsoever. If you believe it to be false, then stop wasting your time going to Church and stop falsely claiming you're a Chris-

Judge Yourself

tian. If you believe it to be true, then make sure your actions align with your belief. Do you *really* believe it? If not, I'd suggest you do some sincere seeking as soon as possible. Eternity is a large thing to gamble with. This isn't a simple matter of perhaps losing several hundreds of thousands of dollars on a bad investment. This is eternal life or eternal death. Live with God eternally or be eternally aware of your separation from God. There's nothing any human has ever experienced that compares with the gravity of this decision.

Our culture fails to teach a complete picture of Christianity. We've kept the parts we like, such as Jesus' perfect love for us as individuals, just the way we are, while ignoring the parts we dislike, such as when Jesus said, "If you love me, you will obey what I command" (John 14:15). We've perverted Jesus' teaching of "Love your neighbor as yourself" (Mark 12:31) to mean we must accept all practices as holy, regardless of any other Scripture references to the contrary. We forget that loving your neighbor is merely the second greatest commandment. The first and greatest is "Hear, O Israel, the Lord our God, the Lord is one. Love the Lord your God with all your heart and with all your soul and with all your mind and with all your strength" (Mark 12:29-30). Jesus put quite a bit more into that first one. All your heart, soul, mind, and strength; with every fiber of your being, you should love God. If you love God, then keep his commands. If you love God, then read the Bible—the words he left for you. If you love God, then seek to understand the truth of what the Bible is really saying on a topic, rather than what you want it to say. If you love God, then spend time with him in prayer.

Love doesn't require blind acceptance of destructive behaviors and beliefs. Out of his love for us, Jesus delivers hard truths. Like the student that needs to understand two plus two equals four before he can advance to more complex calculations, there are things we need to understand before we can progress to a deeper understanding of and closer relationship with God. This holds true for people that are currently believers as well as those who are not. Those who are believers should continually be drawing nearer to God. Those who are not believers will hopefully gain a better understanding of God's perfectly loving, just, and merciful nature, hopefully leading them on a path to salvation.

The early church leaders followed Jesus' example and denounced many sinful practices and individuals. One such example is found in Paul's first letter to the church in Corinth. Paul says, "It is actually reported that there is sexual immorality among you, and of a kind that does not occur even among pagans: A man has his father's wife. And you are proud! Shouldn't you rather have been filled with grief and have put out of your fellowship the man who did this?" (1 Corinthians 5:1-2). Paul doesn't say we should celebrate the behavior. He doesn't say we should accept the behavior. He doesn't even say we need to tolerate the behavior. Paul's instruction is clear. This offender needs immediate discipline. The form of discipline is the highest the church has to offer: excommunication. It's important to note here that this excommunication (and any other church discipline) should always be administered with the goal and hope of repentance and the salvation of the offender (see 1 Corinthians 5:5).

Get Your Stuff Together

Now that we've come to terms with the fact that we "all have sinned and fall short of the glory of God" (Romans 3:23), and have acknowledged that the amount we fall short is infinite, what do we do about it? Our inability to measure up to God doesn't excuse us from trying. In fact, becoming more like God pretty much sums up the entire reason we're even here. Peter says as

Judge Yourself

much: "Therefore, prepare your minds for action; be self-controlled; set your hope fully on the grace to be given you when Jesus Christ is revealed. As obedient children, do not conform to the evil desires you had when you lived in ignorance. But just as he who called you is holy, so be holy in all you do; for it is written: 'Be holy, because I am holy'" (1 Peter 1:13-16).

Dr. Neil deGrasse Tyson is widely known for his work in the realm of astrophysics. His knowledge, personality, and demeanor captivate television audiences. Now I'm no expert in astrophysics, but it's obvious by listening to him that the man possesses a degree of intelligence. Tyson would be an excellent mentor for anyone aspiring to be an astrophysicist. However, it would not be advisable to expect Tyson's mentorship to bring your gymnastics ability to an Olympic level. While excelling in astrophysics, we never hear of his parallel bars exploits or how he nailed a new tumbling routine. Jesus instructs us to make disciples (Matthew 28:19). A disciple is a student. Naturally, if someone is your disciple, then that makes you the teacher—the role model. The term we like to use nowadays is mentor. No one chooses a role model they know doesn't succeed.

Doing our best to eliminate sin from our own lives helps give power and authority to our witness" (1 Peter 2:11-12). This is our duty as Christians; our duty as followers of Christ. Like Dr. Tyson, we must spend time honing our area of expertise. His overwhelming knowledge of astrophysics didn't come quickly and we shouldn't expect different results from our endeavors in Christian discipleship. In our Christian walk, we should aim to be like the Neil DeGrasse Tyson of astrophysics, rather than the Neil DeGrasse Tyson of gymnastics.

Conclusion

We are imperfect beings and we will never make it to perfection on this side of eternity. Nonetheless, we are expected—even commanded—to judge. We must first judge ourselves. We must remove the plank from our own eye, then proceed to our brothers and sisters in a humble, gentle, and loving manner. "Better is open rebuke than hidden love" (Proverbs 27:5).

We must keep in mind that this is a two-way street. We may be on the receiving end of this type of rebuke from time to time. We should be open to the criticisms of friend and foe alike. Friends, of course, want what's best for us. These are criticisms that may hurt, but are designed to bring us to loftier heights in our spiritual journey. But the criticisms of foes can also be just as life-giving at times. Although these are usually designed to inflict pain, we may be able to glean important information about ourselves at the core of their sharp message.

The command to judge ourselves is one that requires constant vigilance. Sin has a nasty way of creeping up on us. Without a constant judging of ourselves, we'll fall into old bad habits and perhaps even new bad habits. "Be self-controlled and alert. Your enemy the devil prowls around like a roaring lion looking for someone to devour" (1 Peter 5:8). If you've aligned yourself with Jesus, then you are an enemy of the devil. And he wants you to fail at every opportunity.

The God we serve is infinitely superior to Satan, however don't let that go to your head. Just because God is able to do something doesn't mean he will. "The Lord said to Satan, "Have you considered my servant Job?" (Job 1:8). Job is the Biblical embodiment of hard times. God let Job, a righteous man, have absolutely everything taken away from him with the exception of his mortal life. God was *able* to intercede, but he was not willing. His purposes were greater than Job's temporary suffering. On the righteousness scale, the Biblical account portrays Job as surpassing most modern-day Christians. If God didn't step in to protect Job from Satan, we can't expect him to do so for us either. God is able, but he will only act in the way that leads to his willful outcome—that which ultimately produces the most good.

Although the devil is full of pride, allowing us to feel superior to him is a tactic he regularly uses. If we feel secure in our own strength, we stop looking inwardly to find our flaws, thinking we've overcome temptation; we've won the war we waged for years or decades. Never stop examining yourself. Where are you weak? Where are you strong? Where do you think you're strong, but you're actually weak? "Do not think of yourself more highly than you ought, but rather think of yourself with sober judgment, in accordance with the measure of faith God has given you" (Romans 12:3).

Always keep watch. In the prepper world, this is called condition yellow. Condition green is when we feel there is no danger and we completely let our guard down, expecting no danger and, further, not looking for the possibility of danger. Condition red is when danger has been noticed and defensive action must take place immediately. Condition yellow is between green and red. Yellow is a state in which there may be danger, but that determination hasn't yet been made. Regardless of whether we expect any danger, we act as though it could arise at any moment. We regularly scan our surroundings to see if anything might pose a threat. Is everything where it should be? Is there anyone acting in a way in which we shouldn't expect a normal person to behave?

Whether we like it or not, Christians are in much more than a battle—we're in a war. There are forces much more powerful than us that want to see us fall. Even if we can never be removed from Jesus' powerful hand (John 10:28), the forces of darkness despise us and want to see us fail at every opportunity. We need to adopt the prepper mindset of always remaining in condition yellow. Every time you realize you've let your spiritual guard down and moved into condition green, willfully change yourself right back to yellow. In this heightened state of spiritual awareness, we're much less likely to fall prey to the devil's schemes.

Author and host of Wretched Radio, Todd Friel, puts it this way: "If you are not making an active effort to try to grow in sanctification—not just not sin—but to grow in sanctification, you will sin and you'll go backwards. Sin is never static. It just never, never is satisfied. It's always going to want more. So, if you're not making ground, you're going to be losing ground."[2]

I recently caught part of an interview of a model on a popular website that shares photos and videos, many of which are explicit. It's quite possible you're thinking of the correct website. Anyway, the young lady was appalled that a man thought the explicit, pornographic acts that women do are bad for marriages and families. She considers herself a Christian, even saying "I'm going to be the type of Christian I want to be."[3] At the end of the segment, she says, "You're choosing to live your life for other people. I'm choosing to live mine for myself."[4] I most definitely don't know this woman, nor do I know any good deeds she performs. I don't know if she regularly attends church or if she prays every day. What I do know is she is attempting to claim the benefits of Jesus' sacrifice with none of the obligation. Jesus says the life of a Christian involves sacrifice (Luke 9:57-62, for example), even saying "No one who puts his hand to the plow and looks back is fit for service in the kingdom of God" (Luke 9:62). What

---

[2] Todd Friel, "Sin Wants You," *Wretched Radio*, June 2, 2023, podcast, 51:52, https://wretched.org.radio/.
[3] whatever, "He Made Her RAGE QUIT?! (STORMS OUT) | Dating Talk #33," November 3, 2022, YouTube video, 03:41:47, https://www.youtube.com/watch?v=cVsgbz0pFIY.
[4] whatever, "He Made Her RAGE QUIT?!"

reason would there be to look back if there isn't something we want? Regarding the case of this young woman, Paul addresses her *exact* thought in 1 Corinthians 6:12-20. The Christian life brings us much freedom, but that freedom is given so we can follow Christ. This type of thinking isn't unique to this woman. Her way of thinking seems to have flooded modern Christianity.

George Barna, author, professor, Senior Research Fellow, and founder of The Barna Group, says 51% of American Christians believe they have a Biblical worldview. Our young lady probably falls into this category. Unfortunately, says Barna, only 6% actually possess a Biblical worldview.[5] That is an exorbitant difference! That's over an 88% error rate! 88% of these people don't understand what they profess to believe. It is simply astounding. Ultimately, this chapter is about you (and me). The moral of this story is we must look at ourselves objectively, determined not to fall prey to confirmation bias. God sees the truth, regardless of what we choose to see. Be open and honest with yourself and God about your shortcomings because you've got plenty of them! Once they're found, work on turning those parts of your life into something that better resembles God.

---

[5] George Barna, *American Worldview Inventory 2021-2022* (Arizona: Arizona Christian University Press, 2022), back cover.

Chapter Eight

Master the Tongue

"Don't lie, cheat, or steal." – Grandma[1]

Did your mom ever say to you, "You've got two ears and one mouth so you can listen twice as much as you talk"? She was trying to tell you you're talking too much. Perhaps you were even missing an important message she was trying to tell you. When I was young, my grandmother liked to hit us with another saying, "If you don't have anything nice to say, don't say anything at all." We see it in kids all the time; always needing to sneak in that last dig. Another of Grandma's favorite adages she would tell us as we were walking out the door every morning was "Don't lie, cheat, or steal." While I'm really not sure if that's a common phrase or not, it was common in her household. One thing I do know, however, is it was good, sound wisdom, likely earned through a lifetime of experience.

Give mom some credit! I don't know your mom, but I know one thing about her beyond any doubt. She's older than you! Duh. Now, age absolutely does not magically grant wisdom, skills,

---

[1] Grandma Seib, *Every Day Before School*, Walking Out the Door, 1995-2000.

good decision-making ability, and whatnot, however older age does equal more time. More time generally means more experience observing the world, both how we affect it and how it affects us. The human brain (yes, moms are human too) is truly a remarkable machine that is constantly learning, even when we may not be consciously aware of the learning process. Time, via experience, develops our minds and allows us to have a more complete, and hopefully more mature, view of the world around us.

Straighten the Rudder

If you've ever spent any time on a motorless boat, you know just how much a small paddle can do. When in motion, kayaks, canoes, and john boats will turn when you put your oar into the water on one side of the boat. Large boats are steered in a similar manner by a rudder, a relatively small paddle at the rear of the ship. When this rudder is turned, despite how seemingly-insignificant its size, the heading of the entire ship is altered. Likewise, the tongue is a small part of the body, but dictates much of that with which the rest of the body must deal. In fact, James uses this analogy in describing the tongue (James 3:4-5). James also compares the tongue with the bit of an animal (James 3:3), and, perhaps more soberingly, to a fire, saying "Consider what a great forest is set on fire by a small spark. The tongue also is a fire, a world of evil among the parts of the body. It corrupts the whole person, sets the whole course of his life on fire, and is itself set on fire by hell" (James 3:5-6).

Your tongue has likely caused more avoidable trouble in your life than any other thing. James also mentions that man has tamed all kinds of creatures, "but no man can tame the tongue. It is a restless evil, full of deadly poison" (James 3:8). I can't promise that you'll gain full mastery over your mouth, but I'm confident that you'll make great strides as you make an honest effort to reign in your tongue. The tongue, indeed, has great power. And as uncle Ben would say, "With great power comes great responsibility."[2]

Let's begin with James' observation of the directional power of the tongue. A small bit in the mouth of a horse or the small rudder of a large ship dictates the course of travel. Likewise, boasts of the tongue can drastically affect the course of one's life. Have you ever had an argument with someone you cared for? Afterward, did you regret anything that you said? Unfortunately, that seems to be the standard human experience. I've always liked the book of Proverbs. It gives a lot of small nuggets of wisdom. As a side note, Proverbs is one of the few places Bible verses are truly meant to stand alone. One such verse is pretty applicable here: "He who guards his mouth and his tongue keeps himself from calamity" (Proverbs 21:23). How much calamity has your mouth brought you?

When we unnecessarily say hurtful things, when we always have to be right, when we talk about people behind their backs, or even when we enter a conversation with an air of superiority over the other person, we're allowing our tongues to guide us down a path we likely don't truly wish to traverse. At least, it's a path that God doesn't want for us. Jesus demonstrates this by saying, "If someone strikes you on the right cheek, turn to him the other also" (Matthew 5:39). If Jesus says this about physical harm, would the command not be expected to apply to instances where no actual harm can be done to us? Another relevant nugget from Proverbs says, "If your enemy is hungry, give him food to eat; if he is thirsty, give him water to drink. In doing this, you

---

[2] Sam Raimi, *Spider-Man*. United States: Columbia Pictures, 2002.

will heap burning coals on his head, and the Lord will reward you" (Proverbs 25:21-22). Kindness, then, rather than harshness, is the best way to get back at someone (not that you should be getting back. Afterall, the Lord says, "It is mine to avenge; I will repay" [Deuteronomy 32:35]).

And now we return to mom's adages. Well, it turns out mom was correct... *again*... (Am I right moms?). James instructs us, "take note of this: Everyone should be quick to listen, slow to speak and slow to become angry" (James 1:19). Two ears and one mouth, remember? Paul goes beyond mom's tried-and-true wisdom and says, "Nor should there be obscenity, foolish talk or coarse joking, which are out of place, but rather thanksgiving" (Ephesians 5:4). This one may sting a bit more. No foolish talk? Makes sense. No coarse joking? That may be difficult, but it's understandable. But no obscenity? Some other translations, including the NASB, use the term "filthiness." No filthy language should come from a Christian's tongue. I know many Christians use profanity, but I believe Paul would caution against doing so.

Mean What You Say

Have you ever said something you wish you hadn't? Or made a promise you chose later not to keep? Perhaps it was less of a choice not to keep the promise and more due to circumstances you may not have had much control over. Maybe the circumstances truly were under your control after all... Regardless of the situation you may be recalling at the moment, I'm sure we've all found ourselves in each of these scenarios at least once in our lives. If not, then it's probably just a matter of time. Our word has seemingly become worth much less than it was in previous generations. Since the time of Cain (see Genesis 4), there have been degenerates in every generation, however it seems there's a pronounced disregard for truth in our current world in comparison with fairly recent history.

Our problem goes beyond a boy and a fake wolf. You remember that one. The kid, playing a prank, told the villagers three times that a wolf had come, yet there was no wolf. When a real wolf arrived, no one believed the child. Non-truths are so prevalent that it's often hard to believe the claims of others. The Christian's life shouldn't be this way.

We've established that honesty is important, but did you know the Bible condones lies? So, we don't have to worry, right? Actually, we had better take a closer look. You knew it wasn't going to be that easy, right? A few places where lying seems excused in the Bible come to mind. Exodus 1 tells how Pharaoh was worried about the growing Hebrew population. Pharaoh issued an order to the Hebrew midwives, saying that all Hebrew males were to be killed immediately after birth. The midwives, obviously caring about mothers and babies, let the children live. When Pharaoh questioned them, they lied and said the women gave birth too quickly for them to arrive. Because the midwives chose to follow God and disobeyed the evil directive, God rewarded them with families of their own (Exodus 1:15-21). On another occasion, Joshua chapters 2 through 6 tell of a Canaanite prostitute named Rahab and her lie to protect Jewish spies. Rahab was rewarded for this act by having her life, as well as the lives of her family, spared when the Israelites invaded the land of Canaan. Rahab also received the honor of being mentioned in what is known as the Hall of Faith in Hebrews 11 (verse 31). These two stories perhaps give the clearest Biblical consent to lie.

The other story I think of is when David acted like he was insane in order to save his life (1 Samuel 21:10-15). Okay, now honestly this story doesn't specify that David actually spoke a lie, but I always imagine that he did. Regardless, there's a crucial element to all of these stories. The Hebrew midwives', Rahab's, and David's lies were designed to protect human life. Have you ever told a lie? I guarantee you have if you're old enough to read this book. But what about recently? Do you lie regularly? Even if your lies are designed to protect innocent people, is it truly their life at stake? Even if it is truly their life at stake, is there honestly (pun anyone?) no alternative other than lying to save their life? I doubt it.

We often tell lies for good reasons; at least, we say they're good reasons. We don't want to hurt someone's feelings. We want to look good to our boss. We don't want to pay full price for a service. We don't want to get caught having forgotten something important. We commonly call these "white lies." As if adding a color to it makes it any better. White is often associated with purity (see Psalm 51:7 as one example among many others), so it's no wonder we would try to use the color to purify a—let's just say it—sinful act. Paul says, "Therefore each of you must put off falsehood and speak truthfully to his neighbor, for we are all members of one body" (Ephesians 4:25).

When we allow these little white lies to infiltrate our speech, we make it harder for those around us to believe everything else we say. Jesus instructs, "Simply let your 'Yes' be 'Yes,' and your 'No,' 'No'; anything beyond this comes from the evil one" (Matthew 5:37). This teaching is repeated in James 5:12. If we pepper our speech with falsehoods, no matter how insignificant, Satan, the father of lies (John 8:44), has a hold on us. Lies of any depth are an invitation for Satan to come into our lives. Moreover, they offer the enemy a rock-solid foothold to combat our witness. If we're known to use lies to make things sound better than they really are, how will non-believers view our message of Christ? What can you say to convince them you're really not lying about this? Afterall, they've already witnessed you lying for something much less lofty than the eternal destination of one's soul. Why wouldn't you also be lying when the stakes have been raised?

Furthermore, Christians are supposed to be... witnesses! If you ever find yourself on a jury, how much belief will you place in a witness that proves to be a liar? What if the witness doesn't blatantly lie, but simply shows a disregard for truth? Obviously, our experience with court witnesses doesn't go forward in time, rather it goes backward into the events the witness... witnessed. Since we can't observe how the witness operates over time, we must listen closely to how they claim to have operated in the past as well as their current verbal and non-verbal communication. If we were to discover through the court proceedings that the witness doesn't answer certain questions, gives delayed responses to others, stalls by repeating questions back to the examiner, or avoids denying direct accusations (some common signs of deception)[3], we will begin to doubt anything the witness might say—*even if what they say is the truth.* As Christ's witnesses, the perception others have of us is important.

Conclusion

How we behave, how we speak, and how we keep our word influence others to either trust what we say or to disregard it as untruth. Remember our untrustworthy court witness? How can we expect to "make disciples of all nations" (Matthew 28:19) if we can't convince others that we have the truth? How can we expect to convince others that we have the truth if we don't follow through with things we say or perhaps worse, if we blatantly

---

[3] Paul Francois and Enrique Garcia, "Studying Liars Part I." December 1, 2011. https://www.tdcorg.com/article/studying-liars-part-i/.

lie? How can we convince others of God's love for them if we constantly engage in gossip? How can we convince others of the Holy Spirit's power to change lives if we never speak a sentence with language that can safely be uttered in a G-rated movie?

At the beginning of time, space, and matter, God spoke everything into existence. With his words, God built everything good in this universe. We are made in the image of God. As God's image-bearers, our words are also very powerful, although not quite on the world-building scale. However, our words can most definitely build or destroy. Paul instructs us, "Do not let any unwholesome talk come out of your mouths, but only what is helpful for building others up according to their needs, that it may benefit those who listen" (Ephesians 4:29).

The words we use matter, regardless of the amount of forethought we put into them. The tongue holds the power to wound or to heal. Unfortunately, the former is often much easier to accomplish. "Do you see a man who speaks in haste? There is more hope for a fool than for him" (Proverbs 29:20). We must carefully consider our words with wisdom and love. Conduct yourself in full knowledge of your position as an ambassador of the gospel (Ephesians 6:19-20). "Don't lie, cheat, or steal;" excellent advice, indeed.

Part Three

Meat

Chapter Nine

How to Read the Bible

"Fragile." It must be Italian." – The Old Man Parker[1]

Advocating a radical change in religious understanding, the apostles seem to have caused a scene wherever they went. After all, the message they carried would drastically affect any practicing Jews and even implicated them in the murder of their own long-awaited Messiah. After getting run out of Thessalonica, Paul and Silas went to another town, Berea, and started preaching. The Bereans not only listened to the message, but they examined it to make sure it lined up with the Scriptures (Acts 17:10-12). Because of this trait, Luke says the Bereans' character was more noble. Like the Bereans, we should consider the religious claims of others, rather than dismissing them for being new or contrary thoughts. Similarly, we mustn't just take someone's Christian teaching at face value. We should make sure it's accurate by studying the Bible. This is much easier if we already have a strong Biblical foundation built by daily reading.

---

[1] Bob Clark, *A Christmas Story*, United States: Metro-Goldwyn-Mayer, 1983.

I'm not one to memorize Bible verses word-for-word. But when I encounter a false teaching, I can often realize it's incorrect simply because I have a foundation already built, even if I can't immediately articulate how exactly the teaching contradicts Scripture. In fact, when I'm trying to make a theological point, I can often remember close enough to how something is worded in order to do a quick internet search to find the exact passage. If you're a verse memorizer, that's perfectly fine. Single verses can be a great source of strength and encouragement. I've just never been particularly good at it. But when memorizing verses, make sure you remember the context of that verse, so that your single-line memorization doesn't make it say something it's really not saying.

Gary, the maintenance guy, was always the first to be called when something stopped working how it should. Today was no exception. After receiving the call, Gary wasted no time. He grabbed the equipment he thought he might need for the job and headed straight to the reported area. Leaving his tools in his truck, Gary went inside to investigate. When Gary arrived at the scene, he took a quick glance and said, "That's not good. The ground's wet." Gary immediately knew what needed to be done. Without saying another word, Gary left the room.

Why did Gary leave the room? From what we know so far of Gary's story, we probably expect that Gary's heading to his truck to grab some tools. What do you think Gary's doing? What is the issue Gary was called to fix? If I were reading this story, at this point, I would think Gary has come across a leak of some sort. Gary may have left the room to disconnect the water or to grab a wet/dry vacuum or some towels before fixing the source of the leak. But this story has almost nothing to do with a leak or any water on the floor whatsoever. But what about the wet ground? This is actually a story about an electrical maintenance call. The ground wire just happened to be the first one Gary could see and he noticed it was wet. Gary left the room immediately without stopping to provide any further explanation because he wanted to turn the circuit breaker off before any further damage might be done.

We intuitively understand what a familiar word means, even when that word has multiple meanings. Ground can be the ground on which we stand, or it could be an electrical ground, or it could be what we did to our coffee beans, or it can mean the consequence for disobeying our parents. The way we know which meaning is being applied is by the context. In the story excerpt above, we know ground is being used as a noun, so we can rule out the coffee beans or a punishment. Since this is a maintenance call, we can assume either the floor is wet or an electrical ground is wet. With the information we have available in the passage, we can't say with certainty which interpretation is correct. We need to read further into Gary's story to come to the correct conclusion that "ground" here refers to an electrical ground.

Ground isn't the only word with multiple meanings. Just to name a few, the words "stand," "trunk," "light," "catch," and "hard" are common in the daily speech of modern Americans. Each of these words has multiple meanings. Words like these are *everywhere* and we don't even realize how often they show up. Yet we seem to deal with them effortlessly in almost all scenarios.

The Biblical writings contain words with multiple possible meanings as well. A translator might choose a meaning based on the context of the original Hebrew, Aramaic, or Greek text. The English word the translator uses might *also* have multiple meanings that don't even overlap with the various meanings of the original word. This has the potential to lead us to a very wrong interpretation of what the writer was actually trying to say. We must pay attention to context. A single verse may not give us all the information we need. In fact, just as we saw with Gary's story, an entire paragraph may not provide enough context. If we read what's happening before and after our passage, we'll typically have a much better understanding of the context of the situation and we'll be better equipped to determine what is truly being said.

Divine Inspiration

We often say the Bible is the word of God. Every word is God-breathed. The Scriptures are inerrant. All of these things are true, but we also need to understand what we mean when we say these things. If the Bible is the word of God and he had control over every word, how did he impart this revelation to each individual writer? Did God physically take control over the writer's body? Did he dictate word-for-word what should be written? While this is possible, I don't think that's how it actually happened.

Each writer with works appearing in the Bible was an individual. Some of these individuals are separated by many centuries. So, we can rule out any sort of Biblical writer's guild or any other sort of collaboration they may have had with the exception of those who were actually contemporaries of one or more of the other Biblical authors. Each author had his own personality. He lived his own individual life. He honed his own individual skills. His education and his contacts were also unique to him. Every experience in his own life culminated in who he was as the writer of his Biblical work. Is there any way he could possibly write something that would be completely cohesive with sixty-or-so other works, separated by hundreds of years? If God didn't directly give every single word, how could this even be possible?

When reading the Bible, it's clear that each writer was unique. Their style of writing and their word choices are not congruent with one another. Yet the messages are consistent across the various books. Rather than stifling each writer with a word-for-word account of what to write, what's much more plausible is God used the experiences, abilities, and creativity of each author to say exactly what God intended. Each writer was inspired by, and surely directed by, God in such a way as to result in the perfect form of the Bible. The form that would best accomplish God's plans.

When we read the Bible, we would be wise to take note of what we know of the author. What is the author's education level? When and where was the text written? What was the culture of that time and location like? The answers to these questions (among others) can help us to understand what the writer means. For example, the word "computer" today conjures a very different image than the same word did just forty years ago. But the newest Biblical writing we have is over 1,900 years old. Obviously a few things have changed in that time. Moreover, if you're not Jewish, you don't share the same culture. Even if you *are* Jewish *and* live in the same area of a Biblical author, you're still separated by thousands of years. Culture, like technology, changes.

Idioms change over time too. A common saying that made sense to someone a hundred years ago could make no sense to someone living today in the same location, let alone on another continent. Even forgetting the time difference, try some of our American idioms with non-native English speakers. If I were to write a letter that made it into a religious text like the Bible, how would it be read in two thousand years? If I were to include an instruction to "leave no stone unturned," would this lead to genuine, heartfelt literal flipping of every stone in the path of the religious followers? Or if I said "It was a piece of cake for Jesus to bring Lazarus out of the tomb," would the studious Christians believe there was a cake involved in this miracle? Was Lazarus' corpse tempted so much by a baked good that it stood up and walked out of its grave? Or perhaps I might write, "Jesus went the whole nine yards on the third day." Now those poor people in the future will think Jesus physically moved nine yards.

What about genre of writing? There are many different types of writing and each is effective under the appropriate circumstances. A detailed treatise on how one should handle specific hardships can be invaluable to people experiencing those situations. An historical account of what happened at a given time can be of immense value to help pattern our lives the same or differently depending on the outcome we want. It can also give us a better understanding of how people felt, and why they felt that way, and why they did what they did. Poetry can convey serious truth, but in a way that speaks to our emotions. We can empathize with how the writer felt in that moment and perhaps find comfort or encouragement for our own lives.

The Bible is a collection of various genres of writing. Have you ever heard the word "epistle" used when referring to some of the New Testament writings? An epistle is basically a letter that is meant to instruct. Many of the New Testament books are epistles. They were letters written to churches or individuals, often addressing specific issues. Technology and culture change, but the nature of humanity itself does not. Since humans are the same now as they were in the first century, there is a lot we can learn from the epistles. Epistles are the most directly-applicable Biblical writings to our modern-day lives.

Think back to the textbook for one of your middle school history classes. A middle school history textbook typically gives an account of the who, what, when, where, how and sometimes even the why for the historical events covered in its pages. What might not be covered in such a textbook is the ethical argument. Why was this action morally wrong? Why was it right? These are questions that often don't get answered in a history book. Historical narrative is another type of writing prevalent in the Bible. Just like a standard history book, these Biblical writings tell us the important details of who, what, when, where, and how, but often leave the moral commentary out. The books of 1 and 2 Samuel are examples of this type of writing.

Another common genre of writing you'll run into throughout the Bible is poetry. Just like the poems you wrote in your high school English class, poetry is typically not the best medium to offer a succinct and exact truth of how things are. Poetry can certainly be used to convey profound, meaningful truths in a straightforward manner, however, poetry really shines in connecting with us emotionally. Poetry allows us to express deep emotions in a manner that might not completely line up with reality in the most literal sense.

We'll use literary devices like metaphor, personification, and even satire to help express our thoughts on a subject. We know "an ocean of people" is likely referring to a large crowd, rather than a bunch of people bobbing around in the Pacific Ocean. We understand that the sun doesn't choose to shine or be covered by clouds. We reason that over-the-top praise for a horrible performance is likely satirical—it means the opposite of what the words themselves say. Alliteration, rhythm, and rhyme help draw us into the world being constructed in a work of poetry. Although the message could be communicated in a more straightforward and direct manner, these literary tools help us understand the thoughts of the writer on a more instinctive, visceral level.

The Bible, through the various times, locations, and cultures of its writers, is the same. We can't approach a millennia old series of documents with only our modern-day preconceptions. We need to seek to understand as much as we can about who was the writer, what was the setting, what style of writing the author chose to employ, and what it was that the author meant to convey with his writing.

Additionally, we can't draw any conclusions about the meaning of any text until we understand the genre of writing. We can't find an article from The Onion or The Babylon Bee and expect nothing but pure, unadulterated truth. If you're familiar with them, then you'll know these companies specialize in satire. Much of the content they produce is just meant to be humorous and doesn't necessarily have any moral leaning. However, some content, although satirical, makes a clear political or religious point.

We're Not the Audience

Jessica wrote a note for her fiancé, Tyler. The note said "I love you! – Jessica." Since Jessica and Tyler work for the same company, Jessica placed the note where she knew Tyler would find it. Unfortunately, Tyler's coworker, Brad, found the note first. Being a good friend of Tyler's, Brad quickly informed him that Jessica had professed her love for Brad. Tyler was rightly upset and immediately confronted Jessica. She tried to explain to Tyler that the note was written for him, but he and Brad knew if that were the case, there's no way Brad could have had the note in his possession.

Hopefully we all see how absurd this story is. Jessica's note was clearly written for Tyler and was inadvertently intercepted on its way to him. Jessica wasn't being unfaithful to Tyler by confessing her love for Brad. Brad just happened to read the note. If Brad had done enough research to know to whom the note was written, he would have been able to properly understand its meaning. Brad could then read the note and learn from it. Brad could read Jessica's "I love you" and understand that Jessica's "you" did not refer to him. He could come out of his reading experience with a deeper understanding of Jessica's relationship with Tyler. The note wasn't written to him, but he could still learn from its contents.

Similarly, the Biblical epistles (letters) aren't written *to* us, but it's probably not an overstatement to say they were written *for* us. The letters were written to specific individuals, churches, or groups of churches and sometimes even include personal greetings and remarks. But the content is still useful for our growth and instruction as the modern church. For example, when Paul says, "Brothers, pray for us" in 1 Thessalonians 5:25, we can rightly conclude that this command is not for us. After all, Paul and his companions have been deceased for over 1,900 years. However, we can still gather from this sentence that we should be praying for our fellow Christians near and far. Just like Brad with Jessica's note to Tyler, we have the opportunity to learn from a message written to someone else.

Correctly Handle the Word

Paul is the most prolific writer of the New Testament, having authored about half of the included works. Even the Apostle Peter viewed Paul's letters as having Biblical authority at the time, saying "His letters contain some things that are hard to understand, which ignorant and unstable people distort, as they do the other Scriptures, to their own destruction" (2 Peter 3:16). Even at this early time in church history, Peter is already equating Paul's letters with Scripture.

Another point in Peter's statement is one this chapter is aimed to combat. Ignorant and unstable people distort the Scriptures. Are you one of these ignorant or unstable people? Have you ever been? If we've spent any reasonable amount of time reading the Bible, then we're guilty of being ignorant and/or unstable on one or more occasions, making the Bible say things it isn't really saying. Remember Tyler's and Brad's incorrect interpretation of Jessica's note from earlier in this chapter? The Bible uses sentences that are much more complex than a simple three-word statement. And as we've already discussed, the culture, location, time, language, experiences, education, and many other things are different from our own culture, location, time, language, experiences, education, and so on.

With all of these barriers between us and the Biblical texts, what hope can we possibly have in coming to an accurate assessment of what the author was trying to say? This whole chapter is about something called hermeneutics. Yes, this entire chapter is about hermeneutics and we're just now mentioning the term. According to Dictionary.com, hermeneutics is:

    1) the science of interpretation, especially of the Scriptures.
    2) the branch of theology that deals with the principles of Biblical exegesis[2]

---

[2] *Dictionary.com*, s.v. "Hermeneutics," accessed July 21, 2023, https://www.dictionary.com/.

This definition leads us to yet another term we should learn. Exegesis is an interpretation of Scripture. Its counterpart is eisegesis, which is an interpretation of Scripture, leaning heavily upon one's own thoughts or biases. Obviously, eisegesis is one we want to avoid. Exegesis is the goal. We want to interpret the Bible how it's meant to be interpreted, rather than how we want it to be interpreted. Brad's and Tyler's interpretation of Jessica's note used eisegesis. They brought their own ideas into the interpretation, rather than letting the text (and all relevant information, like we've been discussing) speak for itself.

Let's move past the abstract idea of hermeneutics and look at some more directly-applicable methods for successfully understanding the Scriptures. When we read the Bible, we need to keep all of the demographic information in mind. Dr. Frank Turek of Cross Examined suggests using an acronym, S.T.O.P. Situation. Type of literature. Object of the passage. Prescriptive or descriptive.[3] Check the context of what's going on and what type of writing is being used. Then see to whom the writing refers, and finally determine if the teaching is instructive or simply describes what happened.

Todd Friel of Wretched.org gives another four-step process. 1) Observation: Observe the text. 2) Interpretation: What does the text say to the original audience? 3) Principlization: What is the principle for all time? 4) Application: How do I apply this text?[4] Similar to S.T.O.P, we see what's going on in the text, including the genre of writing the author is using. We then seek to understand what it is the original audience would have thought the writer meant. Then we look for any lasting principles that would

---

[3] Cross Examined, "How to STOP to interpret the Bible," January 23, 2020, YouTube video, 04:06, https://youtu.be/WhZsSQLf7wc.

[4] Wretched, "Four steps of interpreting Scripture," December 24, 2018, YouTube video, 05:23, https://youtu.be/-Wvt8LTAdaw.

hold true for the time and culture of the writing *and* today. Then we look for ways we can apply the principle(s) to our own individual lives.

There are many other great four-step, or five-step, or six-step processes in the world of Biblical hermeneutics. Feel free to choose one that seems to stick with you. There's a wealth of information available on the topic of hermeneutics. Some are elegantly laid-out in books or online courses. There are also a lot of really good, free resources on the internet. As you look at the various processes, you'll notice very similar steps in each.

We've discussed the need to know the context of any Biblical writing we study. So, just how are we supposed to do that? Fortunately, we don't need to attend seminary or get a degree in Biblical Studies. In fact, we don't need any formal training at all, although that's not to say it wouldn't be beneficial. We live at a time in which we have a much greater understanding of the Biblical text and history than most of the original audience. We have the benefit of archaeological discoveries to help piece together the history of what actually occurred. Living two-thousand-or-more years later, we've also been able to build upon the collective knowledge and wisdom of all those who have gone before us. Obviously, we can learn from the various writings of wise people throughout the centuries if we want to pursue those direct sources. But nowadays, we can also read, listen to, or watch our modern smart people add their wisdom to that which was passed to us.

About that question, "how do we know the context without extensive study?" Our time is valuable and we shouldn't seek to learn everything for ourselves. That's just a good lesson for life. It's the "do as I say and not as I do" or the "learn from my mistakes" lesson. We don't have to learn everything firsthand. We should use the knowledge of others that's available to us. When speaking about "everyday Christians" studying the Bible, I can't think of a better resource than a study Bible. Find one that you like. Look for reviews—the more, the better—to see which appears to be the most accurate and unbiased. We generally want a study Bible that will give us more facts than interpretation of the Biblical text. Most study Bibles will include things like maps of various time periods and paths travelled in Scripture. They also often include timelines with important dates, such as when someone was born or died or when a city was captured. They might include a small concordance to help with word studies. They sometimes graph out Scriptures that seem to complement each other. Perhaps most useful, they typically give some general context of each book, usually including date written, author, audience, key points in the text, etc. They may also give an introduction to the book to summarize what is being written and why it's being written. Be alert for what is fact and what is opinion. Opinions can be a good thing, but don't treat them with the same level of authority as the Biblical writings themselves.

Conclusion

The Bible is divinely inspired. It is the Word of God. It is inerrant. There are no mistakes in God's original Word. When we approach Scripture, we need to keep in mind that it is correct. This by no means should assure us that *we* are correct in our interpretation of what's being said. The Bible is inerrant, but we are not. There are no true contradictions in Scripture. If our interpretations of two passages are in conflict with one another, then one or both of our interpretations are incorrect. This may be due to missing an important piece of contextual information or simply a faulty translation.

Just like no two individuals today are exactly alike, each of the Biblical writers is unique. Each one has his own past experiences that color his writing. His education level helps guide the sophistication and complexity of his words. The time he chose to write brings its own baggage. Wars, political turmoil, and weather events shape his thoughts. He selected a specific genre of writing for each passage he penned, drastically altering the precision and applicability, as well as the feel and emotional capacity of the writing.

God inspired the writer, but he did not dictate the writer's words. Instead, he used every piece of that writer's life, culminating in its perfect usage in crafting the Bible. The writer was autonomous, but God's providence would not let him faulter. Just as in our own lives, God used every experience, good or bad, to result in good. In our own case, we may not always see the good that results, however in the case of the Biblical writers' lives, we get the benefit of their hardships. The good that resulted, at least in part, was their Biblical writing that has blessed the church for thousands of years.

In the Biblical text, we see detailed accounts of laws, genealogies, boundaries, wars, and political events. These passages may not always tell us what to think about the topic. They're not necessarily prescriptive. Even though they're not directly teaching us, when reading these descriptive passages, we can still learn from them. We can learn of God's unchanging nature. His character is good and just and merciful. We can learn of God's sovereignty and of his power. We can learn what was going on in the world when a Psalm was written. We can learn the relationship between Israel and various nations. We can learn who begat whom and understand how that relates to Christ.

We also come across a great deal of poetry throughout the Scriptures. Poetry can contain and convey profound truth, however where poetry really shines is in how it connects with its readers. The poetry we find in the Bible at times helps us to understand God's goodness, power, and wisdom. At other times, it helps us understand our own life experiences better, often directing us back to a focus on God. While its language is sometimes not the most accurate, Biblical poetry offers a much richer understanding of Biblical principles and allows us to feel much closer not only to our brothers, the original authors, but much closer to God.

If you would like to dive deeper into the world of Biblical hermeneutics, there's much more to learn. In this chapter, we've discussed three major types of writing presented in the Bible, but there are more categories that can help correctly determine what a particular passage means. Learning just what we've covered here will make you a much more competent student of the Bible. You are likely now better equipped to accurately interpret the Bible than most Christians that attend church every Sunday. Put your new skills to work! The more you practice, the better you'll get. And you'll gain confidence to stand for what you know is true.

The most important thing to remember is we must exegete! We mustn't seek to make the Bible agree with us. Instead, we must form our ideas about the Bible around the Bible. Remember Brad's and Tyler's bad interpretation of Jessica's simple note. If they had applied just a little of their already-existing knowledge of context, they could have correctly deduced that Jessica's note was meant for her fiancé, rather than his coworker. The Bible is much more complex than Jessica's note, so we must approach it with greater care. Get a reliable study Bible. Pay attention to the context. We must forget what we want and seek to know the truth instead.

Chapter Ten

Be Content

"Correlation does not imply causation." – Dr. Lynette Taylor[1]

Nonstop bickering. Back and forth, each child needs to get the last word in. Each one needs to win the argument. It's easy for an adult to see that it really doesn't matter who wins the argument. It doesn't matter who played with whose toy. It doesn't matter who touched whom last. It doesn't matter who got to go out with their friends yesterday and who can't today. Clearly these things have no lasting repercussions. The child likely won't even remember the conflict in a few days.

Although we see these situations objectively, it's not so clearcut for our children. In fact, it's not so easy for us either when it was our toy that someone else used. What about when we're forced to work with *that* employee? Or when we don't get the vacation days we requested? Worst of all, what goes through our minds when our spot at church is taken? Janice knows that's been MY seat for ten years! Okay, that last scenario may have been a bit dark for some audiences.

---

[1] Dr. Lynette Taylor, *Any Chance to Use the Phrase*, Kentucky Wesleyan College, 2007-2009.

The maturity we gain from growing up and gaining life experience doesn't grant any immunity from this plague. We are never content. "Thou shalt not covet..." (Exodus 20:17 KJV); the 10th commandment inscribed by God on Moses' stone tablets deals with jealousy related to possessions and relationships. Three-and-a-half millennia later and we still can't stop comparing our lives with those around us. Jobs, spouses, children, cars, houses, boats, phones, electronics—We even compare long hours at work and wear the added stress and lack of sleep as a badge of honor. Positive or negative, we want to be the best. And we always fall short.

Toward the end of his Gospel, John records some dialogue between Peter and the risen Christ. Jesus reveals a bit to Peter about how he would eventually die. This is really a beautiful message in itself when Jesus tells Peter, "Follow me!" (John 21:19), fully knowing that Peter would eventually die by crucifixion. John was present at this time, so Peter then asked Jesus how John would die. "Jesus answered, 'If I want him to remain alive until I return, what is that to you? You must follow me'" (John 21:22). John actually ended up dying several decades later, so we now know it was well before Jesus' return. Regardless, it wasn't something with which Peter really needed to concern himself. Peter's responsibility was to follow Jesus and not worry about what other people did.

We have an expression: "Keeping up with the Joneses." I don't know who the original Joneses were, but we never can seem to keep up with these figurative Joneses. With the increase of social media, the pressure is even more intense. Everywhere we look, we see the success of other people. Someone bought a house. Someone got a new car. Someone got married. Someone got a degree or got a new job. People flaunt the best things happening in their lives and we just can't seem to match their success. But that doesn't seem to keep us from feeling like we should.

"Better to be a nobody and yet have a servant than pretend to be a somebody and have no food" (Proverbs 12:9). In the United States, we often feel much poorer than we actually are. We fail to see the big picture and even neglect to notice all that we possess. The Pew Research Center enlightens us, saying "On a global scale, the vast majority of Americans are either upper-middle income or high income. And many Americans who are classified as 'poor' by the U.S. government would be middle income globally."[2] We often spend more money on chasing after those Joneses than we should.

We should be careful to observe that we do "have a servant" in a modern sense. We can afford to pay for everything a servant did when the Proverb was written. Times have definitely changed, but we still have servants. We pay someone to make our food, we pay someone to deliver our groceries, we pay someone to fix our car, we pay someone to make our clothes, we pay someone to do our taxes, we pay someone to cut our hair, we pay someone to do our nails, we pay someone to wash our car, and we even pay someone to wash our dog. Our list of servants is very long. Better to continue having and benefiting from those servants prudently than to squander our wealth seeking the approval of others.

King Solomon poured his life into his work and amassed vast amounts of property, saying, "I denied myself nothing my eyes desired; I refused my heart no pleasure. My heart took delight in all my work, and this was the reward for all my labor. Yet when I surveyed all that my hands had done and what I had toiled to

---

[2] Rakesh Kochhar, "How Americans compare with the global middle class," July 9, 2015, https://www.pewresearch.org/fact-tank/2015/07/09/how-americans-compare-with-the-global-middle-class/.

achieve, everything was meaningless, a chasing after the wind; nothing was gained under the sun" (Ecclesiastes 2:10-11). I don't know the conversion rate for 10th century BC livestock to modern-day U.S. dollars, but there is no doubt this dude had the means to buy any material possession he wanted. See 2 Chronicles 9:13-28 for a glimpse of Solomon's fortune. Solomon, indeed, was the epitome of the Joneses. Yet even at the height of power, fame, and worldly possessions, Solomon didn't find lasting joy or fulfilment.

Our credit card debt really tells the tale. In quarter one of 2013, credit card balances were at $0.66 trillion. Ten years later, in quarter one of 2023, they reached $0.99 trillion.[3] You might say, "But we've had a global pandemic and record inflation over the past few years. This comparison isn't fair!" But the data also show an increase in the years leading up to the pandemic. In fact, I would argue, our spending *is* a pandemic. Regardless, we're focusing on things we don't need to be focused on. Instead of focusing on "Why does Sarah get a new car when I can't afford it?", or "Why should Rachel get married before me?", or "Why does Alex always get away with that, but I can't?", we should focus on Christ. Peter didn't need to know the details of John's life; he needed only concern himself with his own path and following Jesus. We should do the same. When jealousy strikes, Jesus says "What is that to you? You must follow me."

Correlation Does Not Imply Causation

Have you ever heard that red cars get pulled over more often than cars of other colors? One common theory is red stands out

---

[3] Federal Reserve Bank of New York, "Household Debt and Credit Report (Q1 2023)," Accessed July 20, 2023, https://www.newyorkfed.org/microeconomics/hhdc.

more, so police are more likely to take notice. There may be some truth to that claim, but which color gets pulled over the most in real-world scenarios? American Auto Insurance tells us white vehicles are involved in the most traffic stops.[4] Why white? Is there a police conspiracy? Do they train new officers to be on the lookout for drivers of white vehicles? Does the color white make cars more aerodynamic, so they're just faster than other cars? I haven't verified police training standards, nor interviewed officers to determine car color preferences. I also haven't researched the science to prove that the color white doesn't make cars significantly faster. However, I believe the simplest answer is probably the most accurate. The most common car color just happens to be… white! A 2020 article claims 29% of new vehicles sold in North America are white.[5] The number 2 spot is only 19% (that's black for ye of curious mind). With such a large lead in market share, it should be no surprise that white also leads the pack in traffic stops.

Our American Auto Insurance article also mentions a study completed in Minnesota. The study found that "men received at least 50% more speeding tickets than women." It also found a correlation between number of tickets and age. Drivers ages 16-25, while accounting for a mere 13% of Minnesota's population, received 33% of the state's speeding tickets. Why the disparity? Are officers on the lookout for men? Do the police want to make every young person's life miserable? The simple answer is no. Young people tend to drive faster (and probably more recklessly)

---

[4] American Auto Insurance, "What Color Car Gets Pulled Over the Most?" July 23, 2020, https://www.americanautoinsurance.com/blog/what-color-car-gets-pulled-over-the-most/.
[5] Emily Delbridge, "What Is the Most Popular Car Color?" April 26, 2020, https://www.liveabout.com/most-popular-car-colors-4160630.

than those with more experience. Likewise, men tend to be more aggressive and take greater risks than women.

One group of researchers put it this way, "Higher risk taking is particularly characteristic for males between 15 and 35 years, the age when intrasexual competition is the strongest."[6] The authors go on to say that "previous data revealed that males have a significantly higher tendency to die in accidents." This increased risk-taking often translates to driving in terms of speed. It's no wonder young males tend to have the highest insurance rates.

NerdWallet shares some statistics via an IIHS analysis of 2017 U.S. Department of Transportation data. In all age groups, males were involved in more fatal crashes per 100 million miles driven. For ages 16-19, males experienced 6.4 fatal crashes compared to 3.3 for females. In the 20-29 group, males were 3.9 to females 1.6. The disparity is less exaggerated, but still significant for the remaining age groups: 1.6 vs 1.1, 1.5 vs 1.0, and 2.8 vs 2.1 for ages 30-59, 60-67, and 70+, respectively.[7]

Now back to the red car issue. Red may be number 2 on the pulled-over list, but Julie Blackley says only 8.6% of cars on American roads are red, placing them in the number six spot. Cars colored white, black, and gray at 25.8%, 22.3%, and 18.4%, respectively beat out red by a wide margin.[8] What's going on here? We certainly can't rule out the possibility of additional

---

[6] Viktória Tamás, Ferenc Kocsor, Petra Gyuris, Noémi Kovács, Endre Czeiter, and András Büki. "The Young Male Syndrome—An Analysis of Sex, Age, Risk Taking and Mortality in Patients With Severe Traumatic Brain Injuries." Front. Neurol. 10 (2019). https://doi.org/10.3389%2Ffneur.2019.2019.00366.
[7] Kayda Norman, "Average Car Insurance Rates by Age and Gender," April 22, 2022, https://www.nerdwallet.com/article/insurance/car-insurance-rates-age-gender.
[8] Julie Blackley, "Most Popular Car Colors," Accessed August 4, 2023, https://www.iseecars.com/most-popular-car-colors-study.

forces at play. Some other factors we could consider are ownership of red cars by age and gender or we could explore type of car by color (are more sports cars red?). However, I think the matter may be a bit simpler. Even if my hypothesis is wrong, the object lesson is still sound and helps to demonstrate the importance of relational factors. Red cars should indeed be easier for humans to spot. Police officers, most of whom are human (weird, right?), will also possess the tendency to take notice of red things. After all, there's a reason many important signs and warnings are red. The answer to the discrepancy, in my opinion, is simply that the prevailing theory is correct. I believe red cars are pulled over disproportionately simply because they're easier to see than other cars due to no fault of the driver (besides, you know, speeding and whatnot).

Take a trip with me; back to my college days. For my bachelor's degree, I majored in psychology. I don't know how she would classify herself, but I always viewed Dr. Lynette Taylor as the "research-oriented" psychology professor at my school. To me, Dr. Taylor seemed well-versed in research practices and tended to teach more of the science-y courses. Dr. Taylor was notorious among psychology students for one phrase that has apparently stuck with me all this time. It's certainly applicable to any sort of scientific research, but it has much greater application than merely research. Dr. Taylor's words are indeed applicable to *your* daily life. Perhaps she used it so much in class because she understands how profound the statement truly is. "Correlation does not imply causation." What does she mean by that? Just because there is a relation between two events—a red car is pulled over, for example—you cannot immediately conclude that the relation is the cause—you cannot infer the car was pulled over because it's red. There are other factors at play and each one needs to be considered individually as well as how each relates to one another.

We see differences in punishment even within the same household. When one child does something wrong, a parent may pursue a different course of discipline than if another child did the exact same thing. This likely doesn't indicate less love for one child than the other. Rather, the parent knows each of his/her children as individuals and has come to learn how the child responds to various forms of discipline. I've seen this firsthand in my own upbringing. What changed the severity of punishment was the perceived value of the punishment. When considering the course of action, the goal was not to cause pain or emotional torture, rather it was to correct an action and produce a positive result for the future.

They're Just Better

It is plainly apparent that some people are exceptionally good at some things they do. The medium of sports certainly provides many excellent examples. The first athlete to come to my mind is Michael Jordan of basketball fame (among other sports). Michael Phelps has also made quite a name for himself with his swimming prowess. In fact, entertainment in all of its forms has participants that rise to the top, most of whom have some degree of abnormal talent. Michael Bay has produced and directed several successful movies, such as Transformers. Michael B. Jordan and Michael Keaton have played famous roles such as Black Panther and Batman, respectively. Keegan Michael Key is another example from the comedy sector. Michael Crichton authored many successful novels, some of which would become source material for other projects, such as the now-beloved Jurassic Park movies. And arguably the most influential member of this list is Michael Jackson, commonly known as the "king of pop."

Undoubtedly, some of these Michaels had access to opportunities that most people do not. However, I suspect that even given the exact same opportunities, I wouldn't be capable of the achievements of many on this list. Perhaps with enough time, motivation, and dedication, I could have risen to the athletic level of Michael Jordan or Michael Phelps. But even if by some miracle I were able to compete with these sports giants, my career would have been cut short due to a joint condition onset in my early 20s. I'm sure Michael Bay has a greater capacity to draw out the best acting from people than I. Michael B. Jordan and Michael Keaton can assume the identity of their character much better than I. Keegan Michael Key has a way with humor that seems to resonate with people on a much deeper level than my own. Michael Crichton has many accomplishments I would love to claim for myself, but I'm afraid he was a much more imaginative man than I am. Michael Jackson had a mastery over his voice I feel I could never match with any amount of practice and coaching. These Michaels are simply better than me.

There's a commercial that bothers me every time I come across it. I think it helps to illustrate a genuine belief held by our society. Southern New Hampshire University claims that "talent is distributed equally throughout the world but opportunity is not."[9] Now, don't misunderstand my feelings here. I absolutely love the sentiment behind this statement. However, my real-world observations—what I have seen and experienced firsthand in life—tell me it's false. There's a southern saying, "bless your heart" (or his/her heart). All you southerners read that quote

---

[9] Pamme Boutselis, "SNHU Affirms Alignment with National Campaign to #SeeAll," September 23, 2019, https://www.snhu.edu/about-us/newsroom/community/snhu-affirms-alignment-to-seeall.

very differently than those in other areas. "Bless your heart" can certainly be a positive thing. When someone does something good for someone else, "bless your heart" is absolutely a valid southern response. The saying also has a much darker side to it. "Bless your heart" is often used as code when you don't like someone. It's a sort of passive-aggressive statement.

Bringing this tangent back in line, there's yet a third southern use of the phrase that I want to mention. "Bless your heart" is used in an endearing way toward people that try hard, but simply cannot perform to adequate specifications. This could be in school, in sports, in work, or in various other life scenarios. Someone that just can't seem to get the hang of a simple task at work, despite their best efforts might receive a "bless your heart" from a senior coworker. While the southerners have developed a catchphrase for their observation, this wisdom isn't unique to the south. All geographic locations universally observe that some people, bless their hearts, just aren't cut out for sports, or acting, or writing, or teaching, or accounting, or research, or insert any other profession that comes to mind. Many times, it takes longer for the individual to learn what everyone else already knows about their proficiency.

Have you ever felt you deserved something more than the person that got it? In the workplace, we often resent peers that receive promotions to higher ranks than we possess. I once had a very strong chance at getting a promotion making around 50% more than my then-current salary. Before getting to the "official interview" step, I withdrew myself from consideration. Why would I pass on such a huge salary increase? While I still think the opportunity was an excellent one, I had other priorities to consider. Time away from family was a huge factor as well as the overall path I wanted my career to take. From this event in my own life, we can see that people are individuals. Individuals make decisions based on their individual needs, wants, and desires.

An outcome that is not equal is not necessarily unfair. The person that received that promotion after I withdrew had less experience than me. Regardless, what grounds did I have to be upset? It would make no sense for me to complain that I don't make as much money as the person that got the job when I was unwilling to perform the job myself. Inequity is not the same as inequality. Correlation does not imply causation. In the example from my personal life, a less qualified person gained a higher title and pay, resulting in inequity. However, there was no inequality present in the scenario. Both the other candidate and I had equal access to the job. The difference is I was unwilling to commit to the different demands of that position, whereas the other candidate continued pursuing the opportunity.

There's More to Life Than Life

Perhaps because this life is all we've experienced, we sometimes mistakenly feel that this life is all there is; that there is no afterlife. Dr. Frank Turek points out this flaw in our thinking, saying we incorrectly assume "God must ensure that all of his goals and outcomes, including complete justice, must happen in this lifetime."[10] Not everything will go well in this life. We've all seen bad things happen to innocent people. Perhaps we've been that innocent person at times, yet the Apostle Paul claims "we know that in all things God works for the good of those who love him, who have been called according to his purpose" (Romans 8:28).

---

[10] Frank Turek, "15 Mistakes We Make Judging God's Morality – Part 1," *I Don't Have Enough Faith to Be An Atheist*, October 7, 2022, podcast, 48:15, https://crossexamined.org/podcasts/.

How do we reconcile the conflict between Paul's statement and the clearly-observed data we personally gather every day from the world around us? It's the afterlife, of course. Dr. Turek gives a great visual of our attitude when we witness injustice in this life, saying "It'd be like reading a novel halfway through and then slamming the novel down and saying 'Look! This thing didn't resolve itself; not a good book. It didn't tie up all the loose ends. The bad guy's still out there.'"[11] The story isn't over yet. Dr. Turek continues, "It's wrong to assume that because injustice occurs in this life and not all injustice has been turned to justice or complete justice hasn't been done that God is not acting."

So, why do bad things happen to good people? I don't know. But God knows. God has an answer for every single bad event. Unfortunately, we may never come to know the answers on this side of eternity. There's a term that is widely used, called the ripple effect. The ripple effect is a way to express how one event, no matter how inconsequential it may seem, can go on to produce drastic change. The term is derived from ripples in water. If you drop something, say a pebble, into a body of water, say a pond, it will produce a ring of small waves, or ripples, around the point of impact. The ripples are often very far-reaching, despite the small size of the pebble that caused them. Something as small as the life of one insect can have a massive ripple effect. Consider these scenarios:

1) A child is bitten by a mosquito carrying the malaria-causing parasite. The child may not have access to modern medical care for whatever reason; too poor, too remote, etc. The child dies. If this person didn't die, he would have grown and become a national leader. With his newfound power, he

---

[11] "15 Mistakes We Make Judging God's Morality – Part 1."

would have devoted himself to genocide of an entire group of people.

2) A child is with her parents. The child's mother sees a mosquito land on the child's arm and immediately smacks it, killing the mosquito before the child is bitten. Unbeknownst to the mother, this particular mosquito was also carrying a potentially-deadly disease. This child will later grow and devote herself to advancing research for curing Alzheimer's disease. This research will vastly improve the lives of millions of people (and an estimated 500,000 more per year[12]).

How about a biblical example? One of the clearest stories of the ripple effect that comes to my mind is that of Joseph (Genesis 37-50). You remember. He's the guy that had the technicolor dreamcoat. Believe it or not, I've actually never seen that musical. Anyway, Joseph had a couple dreams that made his brothers upset. He dreamed that all of his brothers (and father and mother) would bow down to him. Now, Joseph was far from the oldest child. In fact, he was almost the youngest of twelve sons (he had an older sister as well). Only one brother, Benjamin, was younger than Joseph. I'm not sure of the age differences here, but how would you feel if your younger brother by several years told you he would rule over you? And so, the brothers conspired and took their opportunity to overpower Joseph and sold him into slavery, expecting to never see him again.

Once a slave, Joseph served his new master, Potiphar, well and enjoyed good standing within the household. Unfortunately for Joseph, his master's wife made sexual advances on him. When Joseph denied the advances, she accused him of the misconduct instead, leading to a long prison stay. Joseph would have

---

[12] "Facts & Stats," Alzheimer's San Diego, accessed July 19, 2023, https://www.alzsd.org/resources/facts-stats/.

expected to remain a prisoner there his entire life, but he was able to befriend the Pharaoh's cupbearer who promised to speak to Pharaoh on Joseph's behalf. Alas, the cupbearer promptly forgot about Joseph... for the following two years. *Finally,* the cupbearer remembered Joseph only after Pharaoh needed someone to interpret a dream. Joseph was summoned and gave the dream's interpretation and was then awarded with power in Egypt second only to Pharaoh himself.

Egypt was pretty much THE power back in the day. To go from a disgraced slave, serving a life sentence in prison to the number two guy in Egypt was unthinkable, let alone doing that in just one day. Joseph went on to prepare the country for a great famine that would last for seven years. Without Joseph's leadership, the entire country of Egypt would have suffered great loss of life. In fact, not only Egypt, but the surrounding lands as well. Joseph's brothers and father came to Egypt during the famine to obtain food that only the Egyptians had, and that only due to Joseph's preparations.

We read Joseph's story of redemption on this side of history. It's clear to us as we read that Joseph's suffering has an end. Not only is there an end to Joseph's suffering, but that suffering actually had monumental purpose. If Joseph wasn't wrongly sold into slavery, he wouldn't have worked for Potiphar. If he didn't work for Potiphar, he wouldn't have wrongly gone to prison. If he didn't go to prison, he never would have met Pharaoh's cupbearer. If he didn't meet Pharaoh's cupbearer, he never would have had the opportunity to interpret Pharaoh's dream. If he didn't interpret Pharaoh's dream, he never would have been given power over the land of Egypt. If he didn't have power over the land of Egypt, countless people would have suffered and died due to the severity of a *seven-year-long* famine.

Be Content

In what is, perhaps, the first direct mention of the effect of the ripple effect (I know this sounds redundant!) in the Bible, Joseph said to his brothers, "You intended to harm me, but God intended it for good to accomplish what is now being done, the saving of many lives" (Genesis 50:20). Even the cupbearer's forgetting of Joseph for two years led Joseph to meet Pharaoh at the exact right time. Instead of simply gaining his freedom as might have happened two years prior, Joseph gained the power to save countless lives. The ripples of Joseph's suffering were far-reaching, indeed.

How about an example from the Scriptures with an outcome that's not so clear? King David; Israel's most beloved king. You know, David was also one of God's favorites. David is known as the man after God's own heart (1 Samuel 13:14; Acts 13:22). As a side note, I've often taken great comfort from David's story. David, like all of us, was human. Humans sin. I bet you've already sinned today (You dirty sinner!). Don't worry though, I have too. Fortunately, God has already made a way for us: "The blood of Christ... [cleanses] our consciences from acts that lead to death, so that we may serve the living God!" (Hebrews 9:14). Reading David's story and understanding the gravity of some of his poor decisions, yet knowing God still held him in such high regard, gives me great hope for myself with all of my own failures and shortcomings.

And now we return to our regularly-scheduled programming. This man after God's own heart, David, sinned in some major ways. Possibly the most notorious of David's sins was the Bathsheba saga. Bathsheba was a beautiful woman that apparently lived near David. Bathsheba was bathing on her roof and David was able to see; and he liked what he saw. David discovered Bathsheba was married and her husband was a soldier off fighting a battle for the kingdom. David proceeded to commit adultery with Bathsheba and one of the potential products of this behavior, a baby, was conceived. David, wanting to hide his sin, brought Bathsheba's husband back from the war effort in the hope that he would sleep with his wife and the baby would be assumed to be his, rather than David's. Unfortunately for David, this man refused to sleep inside his home, knowing his comrades were still fighting a war that he should be part of. Still desperate to hide his actions, David decided to go even deeper into the forest of sin. David had his army commander place him in the area with the most intense fighting, then withdraw from him so he would be killed in battle. David's plan worked. In fact, because of this scheme, even more of David's men died in battle.

Bathsheba mourned her husband's death and David took her as his wife after the mourning period. "But the thing David had done displeased the Lord" (2 Samuel 11:27). Nathan the prophet confronted David regarding this incident. Once David realized how truly terrible his sin was, he immediately sought the Lord's forgiveness. This, by the way, is the model we should follow. When David came to terms with his sin and admitted it to himself, he immediately turned to God (read Psalm 51 for David's prayer following this event). David's sin was forgiven, although the consequences remained. *When* you sin, turn right back to God. Don't be deceived into believing your sin can't be forgiven.

David's actions rippled forward. Unlike the ripples caused by Joseph's brothers, David's ripples caused death. Even worse, the death caused was that of an innocent life—David's unborn baby. David's sin was forgiven, but the consequences (God's punishment) remained. David's first son by Bathsheba died just seven days after birth. Now not everything here need be negative. I want to assert a potential positive ripple out of this whole debacle. David's second son through Bathsheba was a guy named Solomon. That's the one. King Solomon; commonly known as the wisest man that ever lived. Solomon's life was a positive ripple from David's sin. Through his reign, King Solomon increased the wealth and territory of Israel greatly. He was also widely known and respected for his wisdom and I'm sure Judaism was spread due to Solomon's words and actions. Much of the book of Proverbs was written by Solomon, as well as Ecclesiastes and Song of Songs (or Song of Solomon). Solomon indeed had a profound effect on the people of his age, but his influence continues today through his written works.

About that potential ripple. David had sons older than Solomon, yet Solomon was the chosen successor to the throne; both by David and God. If Solomon had an older brother by the same mother, this already-messy succession plan could have been increasingly more difficult by an order of magnitude. At least two of David's other sons, Absalom and Adonijah, were killed as a result of Solomon's succession. Adding another son through Bathsheba could certainly have added to the death toll; and not just the life of the individual. He may have had a following, creating a civil war (similar to Absalom's story).

Let's consider a newer example from the Bible. At times, the Apostle Paul was kept from going places he wanted to go. Paul wrote a couple letters to his protégé, Timothy, that we have the privilege of having preserved in the New Testament. Timothy was a young church leader and Paul's letters to him offered a lot of advice for his leadership role. The church has benefited greatly from Paul's wisdom over the past two millennia. In the first of these letters, Paul says, "Although I hope to come to you soon, I am writing you these instructions so that, if I am delayed, you will know how people ought to conduct themselves in God's household" (1 Timothy 3:14-15). Paul had experienced enough unexpected events through his travels to know that delays happen. Sometimes delays even become nevers. In Romans 15:24,

Paul expressed his desire and intention to go to Spain to spread the gospel message, but it's unclear if he was ever able to make that journey. Because Paul knew delay was a possibility, he wrote a good, detailed letter to Timothy that has been preserved for our benefit today.

Perhaps more importantly than the book of Timothy, Paul wrote the letter to the Romans because he was continuously unable to go to Rome. "I do not want you to be unaware, brothers, that I planned many times to come to you (but have been prevented from doing so until now) in order that I might have a harvest among you, just as I have had among the other Gentiles" (Romans 1:13). The book of Romans is arguably the most important book in the New Testament. Paul gives a clear explanation of the gospel message. This is the core of Christian faith. Romans argues for the simplicity and severity of our belief and faith in Jesus. We're saved by faith through nothing but the grace of God, regardless of any good (or bad) works we may ever perform. See chapter 2 for more on the gospel message. If it weren't for the acts of God and Satan to prevent Paul from travelling to Rome, we never would have had such a clear apostolic defense of the gospel message. Paul—likely frustrated, having never known the reason—was kept from doing the good thing he wanted that would have saved perhaps hundreds of souls in Rome and instead wrote a letter that has saved hundreds of thousands, if not millions, of souls since then.

Here's one last ripple example from the Bible; and this one is huge! "In the beginning God created the heavens and the earth" (Genesis 1:1). Okay, that would obviously be a big ripple, but that's actually not the one we're using here. After God put all of creation together (time, space, light, water, land, plants, animals, humans, etc.), the caretakers of the planet, Adam and Eve, lived in Eden with the Lord. You know the story of the serpent deceiving Eve (Genesis 3). Eve ate of the one tree that was forbidden, the tree of the knowledge of good and evil, and gave some to her husband, Adam, who also partook of the fruit. I don't know about you, but eating a piece of fruit doesn't typically top my day on memorability. The action was certainly sinful since both Eve and Adam knew it was forbidden by God, but I doubt either truly thought the consequences would be so significant. Eating this fruit that day has rippled forward, affecting literally every single human to ever exist. Everything bad in your life is a ripple from Adam and Eve's one act of disobedience millennia ago. Now before you try to blame your ancestors for all the evil in your life, consider that you may not have existed if sin had never entered the human race. There are what seem to be an infinite amount of good and evil ripple-causing events that brought you into being and God uses evil events for good purposes. And your life is certainly a good purpose!

Sometimes the only effects we can clearly see are the negative ripples. We can speculate at what might have been, but we don't have the means to discern the future (or potential futures, for that matter). However, we're fortunate to know that everything—all awkward and uncomfortable situations; all mockery, insults, and ostracism; all sickness, pain, and death—are leading to a good outcome (Romans 8:28). I came across a video several years ago that beautifully put suffering into perspective. I wish I could remember the source. First and foremost, I would love to watch the video again, myself. Additionally, I would love to give credit to that person.

The man is on a stage with a large whiteboard. He starts by putting a dot on the left side of the board. This is your birth. He draws a line from that dot and stops to add another dot. This dot is a point of suffering. Imagine the worst thing that's ever happened in your life. You don't have to shy away from the tough stuff. Death of one or more important people in your life, abuse, rape, slavery; put the hardest thing you can think of at this point. Now let's say this happened when you were 20-years-old, so that's the age of this dot. Our presenter continues the line, stopping in ten more years. At 30-years-old, does that trauma still matter? Perhaps it does. The line continues. At 40-years-old, how does the trauma affect you? Any less than the previous dot? The line continues. At 50? What about 60? 70? If you live to be 80-years-old, is that trauma still more vivid, exactly as vivid, or less vivid than it was 60 years ago?

I'm sure we can all agree that the trauma is less intense now than it was at 20. That's not to say it doesn't have lingering effects. Major psychological trauma indeed has a nasty tendency to stick around in our minds. But as the saying goes, time heals all wounds. The scar may still be there. The nerves and skin may not have healed quite like new, but some amount of healing has certainly taken place over 60 years. Perhaps you die at 80-years-old. This dot is the last in your life. Nonetheless… the line continues. Remember, "Multitudes who sleep in the dust of the earth will awake: some to everlasting life, others to shame and everlasting contempt" (Daniel 12:2). "Everlasting" is quite some time. This is no gobstopper that makes empty promises of forever-flavor. This is a true eternity. Never-ending life. As your line continues an additional 60 years, how does that trauma affect you? After a hundred more. Is it still sad? Are you still angry after five hundred years? Are you still afraid after eight thousand years? Add as many zeros as you can comprehend to this number and you haven't even scratched the surface of eternity. Even if every single moment you lived in your mortal flesh was absolute and utter misery, all things will be made right. We are eternal beings; just trapped in a mortal viewing chamber.

The story of Shadrach, Meshach, and Abednego (in Daniel) is a common one in Sunday school classes, and for good reason. It really is a wonderful demonstration of God's power. Perhaps even more importantly than that, it gives us an excellent example of a proper attitude regarding God's power. The Israelites were captive in Babylon. The three Hebrew men were servants of the king, Nebuchadnezzar. The king made a gold statue of himself and ordered everyone to worship it. Naturally, the three Hebrews refused. When Nebuchadnezzar confronted them, threatening to throw them into a furnace, the steadfast men replied, "If we are thrown into the blazing furnace, the God we serve is able to save us from it, and he will rescue us from your hand, O king. But even if he does not, we want you to know, O king, that we will not serve your gods or worship the image of gold you have set up" (Daniel 3:17-18). This response is truly astounding. Shadrach, Meshach, and Abednego fully knew that the king was not making an idle threat. Nebuchadnezzar would undoubtedly follow through on his promise, yet they would not put any other gods before the one true God. This in itself was very impressive, however the thing that's perhaps most comforting is the "even if." The men knew God had the power to save them. They even *expected* God to save them. But "even if" he chose not to save them, they knew they needed to do the right thing, deferring to God's judgement of the situation (ripples included).

My son, now two-years-old at the time of this writing, is really a happy, carefree guy. He's great. However, there are times (many each day, in fact) that he is absolutely distraught over his life's circumstances. He can't go into a room that he wants. Or he can't have the snack he wants. Or he can't carry his syrupy pancake around the room. Or it's bedtime, but he wants to continue playing. I'm sure any parent can relate. The simplest things are devastating for a young child. Yet, we grow and learn that life is more complex than restricted areas, snacks, and bedtimes, and, while these things may still be a nuisance at times, they no longer stop us in our tracks. We can move on from them and focus on more meaningful things, like girls or boys.

Teenagers are often obsessed with the opposite sex. Usually there's one particular object of fancy. Although next week, that object might be a different person. When the crush is obviously not interested and there's no hope of a gf/bf situation, the teen is devastated. Their life is most definitely over. Romantic feelings aside, teens often place high value on social perception. Any public mistake is the end of the world and will be remembered for the rest of time. In fact, this mistake will be the main topic of conversation every day for those who witnessed it for the rest of their lives. Of course, we again grow and learn that life is more complex than whether one individual is attracted to us or whether we made a mistake today or not. We learn that there are many fish in the sea and one of those fish is probably a better fit for us than this one. We also learn that mistakes happen every day by every person and people really don't care that you messed up. It will be forgotten after a while.

So, what is devastating in your life now? Perhaps it's still a girl or boy. You know, we often grieve over the same things we did as children and teens; hopefully we at least have a better perspective on it now though. Perhaps your romantic life is squared away, and now your focus has changed to your finances. Is that debt consuming your thoughts? What about your job? Boss is erratic or unreasonable? Is that a tumor or are you just being overly cautious? Are you going to end up with that heart condition your dad has? Why can't you stick to your diet and exercise plan? Hopefully as adults we can step back and see these issues like our child's undesirable snack problem; It's not the end of the world. Perhaps we need to buckle down and finish our meal first, then we can have the snack we want. For example, we might stop eating out to save money (finish the meal) so we can pay off our debts (the snack).

Nonetheless, our worries often still get the best of us and we regularly feel that it's the end of the world. It's the end of the world because our home is foreclosed on and we'll be homeless forever. Or perhaps we feel our marriage is irredeemable or our career is destroyed. You know what? These things may be true, but none of them are the end of our world. Life continues and we can be redeemed from our mistakes. It's easy for me to say that from my safe position, but it feels very different when you're in them; just like it does to my son when I take a dangerous object away from him. I take it away for his benefit, but he absolutely doesn't see it that way. Eternity is indeed a long time. In fact, that statement, although it conveys my meaning well, is perhaps misleading. Eternity is outside of time. Eternity never begins, nor ends. It really is too much for us to fully comprehend while we're stuck inside of time. When we're freed from our mortal vessels and bestowed with immortality, perhaps then we will grow and learn that life is more complex than finances, careers, and health issues.

Conclusion

The next time you feel your lot in life is unjust for whatever reason, remember that there are many factors at play. Is our red car truly being targeted or is there another force working against the result we expected? Sometimes our red car is indeed the target. Sometimes we miss out on opportunities simply due to who we are. Things like our age, gender, religious beliefs, or even the color of our skin can certainly affect events beyond our control. It's important not to dwell on what we can't change, but instead focus on what is within our power. Things like who we hang out with, or how we treat other people, or how much effort we put forth in education or work are much more valuable uses of our time. We need to pose Jesus' question to ourselves, "What is that to me? I must follow Christ."

Despite our best efforts, we will fail—a lot. We just need to face the facts that someone is better than us. Period. No "buts." That's just how it is. Someone may practice a craft for 10,000 hours and still not compare to someone with far less practice. Nature, nurture, and just plain luck (or God's providence) all have a say on our successes.

The common perception seems to be that becoming a Christian is supposed to make our earthly lives perfect. No more trouble can befall me because I have Jesus! Alas, the cold, hard truth is God promises our lives will contain trouble. Jesus, just after telling the disciples of his death and their subsequent scattering out of fear, didn't tell them what they necessarily would have wanted to hear. Instead, he promised them trouble. This life is riddled with trouble, but Jesus brings about our ultimate victory. He has overcome (John 16:33).

Indeed, sometimes one's faith brings an increase in trouble. See Foxe's Book of Martyrs for some real, historical examples of people whose Christian faith brought about worldly trouble. Take solace in knowing that God has the power to change any situation, but keep the right attitude toward his power. When the world seems against us, we can take solace, just as Jesus did, in knowing we're not alone. Our Father is with us (John 16:32).

God's wisdom is infinitely vaster than our own. He knows the full extent of every ripple from the beginning to the end. Nothing escapes his view. Sometimes in his wisdom, God does not intervene when and where and how we think he should. "But even if he does not," serve him, follow him, and trust him.

Chapter Eleven

As in the Days of Noah

"Do I need to be liked? Absolutely not! I like to be liked. I enjoy being liked. I have to be liked. But it's not like this compulsive need to be liked, like I need to be praised." – Michael Scott[1]

Have you ever not realized something that everyone else did? It was so obvious to everyone but you. When you finally figured out what everyone else already knew, how did you feel? Foolish? Insincere? Uncaring? From as early as I can remember, my grandmother made stewed apples. I loved them! I asked for them all the time. Have you ever heard of stewed apples? Of course you haven't. It wasn't until I was probably around twelve-years-old that I learned that isn't what they're called. You see, *stewed* apples are those wonderfully sweet, cinnamon-y apples, similar to what you might find inside an apple pie or served alone at a restaurant like Cracker Barrel. Listen, teach your kids proper

---

[1] *The Office*, season 4, episode 1, "Fun Run," directed and written by Greg Daniels, aired September 27, 2007, https://www.peacocktv.com/watch/playback/vod/GMO_00000000007428_01/41f1443a-a633-3618-a85f-cbcfca438e31?paused=true, 00:11:28.

words! Being around twelve-years-old and realizing I was inadvertently using baby talk was embarrassing.

Now, let's turn it around. Have you ever been the only one to realize something that no one else does? Even worse, did they refuse to listen to your reasoning when you explained your well-intended logic? Sometimes people get upset when you tell them they're wrong, regardless of your intentions. Having been a manager of several teams for different companies over the past thirteen-or-so years, I'm well accustomed to having to follow budgets. Typically, the most important budget is for staffing; the number of hours employees work. On one occasion, my boss said we were drastically over budget and needed to figure out how to cut hours. Of course, this tip off came from those above. After our conversation, I went straight for the data in order to figure out how we had gotten so far off course while following the same staffing pattern. I discovered that our budget had been cut by over ten percent for the current month. The programs we used didn't give that answer directly, so it took a little simple math. Upon my discovery, I tried to tell my boss, but was met with immense resistance and an unwillingness to look at the data. I was told we just had to make it work.

Around a month later, after cutting our staff to the bone and still being over budget, my boss came to me and said the regional manager discovered that there was an error. Our monthly budget had been cut way more than it was supposed to be. The amount? Around ten percent. I of course felt immense relief that the truth was finally known and acknowledged. Perhaps I should have taken the "I told you so" route, but that's typically not my style. I believe my initial response was a simple "yup." I still don't know if my boss ever realized that I pointed out the exact error a month earlier. This could have been a hero moment, my boss bringing the error to the attention of those with the power to make the correction. Instead, not acknowledging the truth led to more stress for me as the manager, but also for every member of our team that had to lose pay when we cut hours, and we can't forget about the additional workload left for those who still had to stay and finish the work.

I'm sure you've experienced this phenomenon in your own life, although perhaps not in terms of a budgeting error. How does it make you feel when no one will listen to the truth? I know it's not a pleasant experience. Having the best of intentions, not only seeking to save myself the stress of cutting hours, but also hoping to protect my employees from losing money and gaining extra stress from the lack of hands, I wanted the truth to be accepted. When my audience refused to even *listen* to the truth, I experienced an array of emotions. Naturally, anger was one of those emotions; "I'm on your side! Why won't you even listen to me?" The other chief emotion I experienced was sorrow for my employees that I would have to send home against their wishes as well as those who had to pick up the slack after I did so. As a side note, be nice to your boss! When they give you bad news like "you have to go home because we're over budget," they likely don't have a choice in the matter and they might be struggling emotionally with the news as well.

When we know the truth and those around us refuse to listen to it, or choose to ignore it, or even worse, attack the truth as false, it's not a fun situation. Our culture is filled with all kinds of evil practices. Some of these practices are more heinous than others. There's even a movement to reclassify pedophiles as "minor-attracted persons," as if changing the label makes the practice more palatable. Yet this word game isn't a new tactic. Nowadays, we change the meaning of words to fit our own agenda. Tolerance, for example, from a dictionary view basically means to accept and permit differences. One could say a person experiences tolerance when their race, gender, origin, beliefs, age, appearance, etc. are overlooked or even ignored in respect to how the person is treated. Martin Luther King Jr. was seeking such tolerance when he uttered the famous line, "I have a dream that my four little children will one day live in a nation where they will not be judged by the color of their skin but by the content of their character."[2] King's dream was the definition of tolerance—to judge each person by *who* the person is, rather than *what* the person is.

"Tolerance" as evidenced by our culture is far from King's vision. "Tolerance" in this sense means much more than accepting the differences in people's backgrounds, appearances, and choices. Rather, this "tolerance" requires outright agreement with and approval of only specific types of lifestyles and beliefs. No longer can we live in peace and respect individual choices; we now must embrace those choices or we're called toxic, bigots, MAGA Republicans, white supremacists, insurrectionists, and I'm sure the list goes on. This "tolerance," you see, is actually intolerance. The term has been completely turned upside down. Tolerance seeks to unify by what we have in common and accept the differences as being unique to that person. "Tolerance," on the other hand, seeks to unify only those who agree—those who hold the same views or background—while dividing those who hold diverse views or backgrounds.

---

[2] Martin Luther King, Jr, "I Have a Dream," (speech, March on Washington for Jobs and Freedom, Lincoln Memorial, Washington DC, August 28, 1963), https://www.npr.org/2010/01/18/122701268/i-have-a-dream-speech-in-its-entirety.

Hot or Cold?

Why is it that so many people want to hold the title of Christian, but want no part in following Christ? To bear the name of Christ, one should pursue a life in accordance with Christ's teachings. In order to pursue such a life, one must *know* Christ's teachings! This is a phenomenon I've never understood. Do they call themselves Christians because they look up to Jesus? Do they see something to gain socially from an association with Christianity? Or, perhaps, do they fear what familial repercussions might take place if they don't profess to be a Christian (with their words, at least)?

I might look up to a master violinist or chef, but I don't then say I'm a violinist or chef unless I practice those arts. Christianity, likewise, is something that requires practice and training. Paul used sports and military metaphors to make this point. A Person cannot be a Christian if they simply claim to be one. There must be a practice of the art. There must be some sort of lifestyle to evidence the profession. Not that any Christian will ever be perfect on this side of eternity, but the effort should certainly exist to become more like the one whose name we bear. Train for the race (1 Corinthians 9:24-27), fight the fight (2 Timothy 4:6-8), endure hardships like the soldier you are (2 Timothy 2:3-4), and reap the rewards of victory (2 Timothy 2:5).

Jesus said to the church in Laodicea, "I know your deeds, that you are neither cold nor hot. I wish you were either one or the other! So, because you are lukewarm—neither hot nor cold—I am about to spit you out of my mouth" (Revelation 3:15-16). There's debate on whether this message was meant for the Laodicean church of the time it was written, or for a period of church history later in time, but prior to today, or for the church at the end of the age. It's absolutely possible that all three are correct. Regardless, there is one thing we can say with certainty about Jesus' statement. He does not like lukewarm Christianity. In fact, Jesus would prefer honest unbelievers—those who make no claim to be followers of Christ—to false believers—those who claim to be Christian for any number of reasons, but fail to produce fruit in line with a repentant life (Matthew 3:8).

Your family cannot save you. Neither can your friends. Your heritage is likewise meaningless in terms of salvation. John the Baptist (not the apostle) was sent to pave the way for Jesus' ministry. To those thinking they were in God's good graces due to their Jewish ancestry as God's chosen people, John said, "And do not think you can say to yourselves, 'We have Abraham as our father.' I tell you that out of these stones God can raise up children for Abraham" (Matthew 3:9).

As evidence of either our general unbelief in the validity of Scripture or perhaps it's simply our complete lack of Biblical knowledge, Americans largely don't believe in hell—or, at least, we don't believe *we'll* go to hell. George Barna says, "It is relevant to point out that Americans generally reject the idea of going to Hell or some place of eternal torment, after their time on earth expires. Currently, just 2% of Americans believe they will experience Hell after they die. That figure has stayed remarkably stable over the last 40 years, fluctuating between 1% and 2% throughout that entire period."[3] We don't like the idea of hell. Admittedly, I don't like it either. Logically, I know that hell has a necessary role due to the infinitely just and infinitely wise God we serve. However, hell is just one of those things my mortal mind hasn't yet quite been able to grasp. In fact, anything eternal is difficult—or impossible—to fully comprehend while still in our mortal shells. But we can trust that God, the infinitely moral,

---

[3] George Barna, *American Worldview Inventory 2021-2022* (Arizona: Arizona Christian University Press, 2022), 82

infinitely good, and infinitely loving being that is sovereign over all space, time, and matter, will do the right thing. It's in his nature. Christians often say that God can do anything, but that's not quite true. God cannot do evil. God is good and he is unchanging. God always has and always will do the right thing.

Jesus spoke much more on hell than he did on heaven. Hell is real and most people will end up eternally separated from God. They will end up in this hell not due to God's poor planning, but of their own accord. On that day, not a single soul will have a solid argument against God. Every person will know the right they did as well as the wrong they did and they will be held accountable to every word they ever uttered (Matthew 12:36). Why did Jesus speak so much about hell? I think it was because in the end times—where we are now—we choose to act like hell doesn't exist. We like to forget that Jesus said, "Enter through the narrow gate. For wide is the gate and broad is the road that leads to destruction, and many enter through it. But small is the gate and narrow the road that leads to life, and only a few find it" (Matthew 7:13-14).

Jesus didn't claim to be one way to salvation; he said he is the *only* way to salvation. "I am the way and the truth and the life. No one comes to the Father except through me" (John 14:6). We can certainly debate what happens to those that never hear the gospel message, but Jesus' statement is clear. There is no other way and Jesus acknowledges that it's narrow. Jesus is the exclusive path to salvation which most people will never take. If you've read everything up to here in this book, then you've been presented with the gospel message. Sorry, but you no longer have the excuse of "I didn't know." There may be multiple people living in your home. If someone knocks on the door, any one of them can open the door and let the guest in. Unfortunately, that's not how your heart works. You are the sole inhabitant. There is no one else to answer the door for you. Jesus is waiting at the door to your heart. "Here I am! I stand at the door and knock. If anyone hears my voice and opens the door, I will come in and eat with him, and he with me" (Revelation 3:20). Will you answer the door?

Those who think they can put off the choice to truly "get right with God," those who we might view to be "on the fence," have already made their decision. There is no fence to be on. You see, it's a path. There's a narrow road and a wide road and you can't take both roads. You're either on the narrow road or you're on the wide road. There is no middle ground. You can't straddle both roads because their paths are divergent; they're headed in opposite directions. In chapter 5, we discussed the matter of our master. We either serve God or we serve the devil. Servitude to the devil often takes the form of self-worship; we put our needs, our wants, and our interests above God. Paul said, "You cannot drink the cup of the Lord and the cup of demons too; you cannot have a part in both the Lord's table and the table of demons" (1 Corinthians 10:21).

Expect Persecution

Is the Christian church being persecuted? The short answer is yes. It perhaps may be easier to see the persecution taking place in other parts of the world where Christians are killed simply due to their profession of faith in Christ. Yes, this does happen today. Fortunately, this is not the case for us in the United States. We still benefit from a great deal of religious freedom, protected by the greatest country to have ever existed. However, we're seeing a growing proclivity for Christian persecution, even in this great nation. Christian belief is daily made out to be the enemy of all that is good, just, and fair. Christianity is seen as the opposite of diversity, equity, and inclusion. Christianity is touted as anti-black, anti-woman, and anti-gay. It's a group of bigoted, misogynistic, heteronormative, cis-gendered, white men who want nothing more than to control the lives of everyone else.

In a speech given shortly before her 2016 presidential campaign, Hillary Clinton uttered some chilling words. Speaking for abortion, Clinton said, "deep-seated cultural codes, religious beliefs and structural biases have to be changed."[4] Seeking to change cultural codes and any sort of biases can absolutely be positive things in the right context. But the government seeking to change religious beliefs is dangerous. By God's providence, American Christians have enjoyed immense religious freedom in this country and that still holds true today. But the tide is changing. The war on Christianity in America is undoubtedly underway. We seek to make God a devil and the devil a god.

Our TV and movies that include Christian-inspired elements display a distorted view of Christianity. *The Handmaid's Tale* is a recent example of a dystopian Christian society where men rule and women serve; or else. God, here, is a devil. The television series *Lucifer* is another recent example of a false view of Christianity. The titular character, Lucifer, is the one that we typically call Satan or the devil. In this series, the devil is elevated as a hero. Our culture uses things like these shows to chip away at God's positive traits and elevate worship of other gods; money, sex, and social standing, for example. Just one such attack couldn't turn the battle around, but the constant, coordinated attack from a unified front certainly seems to have made a massive impact over time. And it's accelerating.

---

[4] Marc Thiessen, "Hillary Clinton's war on faith," *New York Post*, October 15, 2016, http://nypost.com/2016/10/15/hillary-clintons-war-on-faith/.

This degradation of Christian doctrine has also deeply infiltrated the supposed church. Pastors have no idea what the Bible says. Even if they do know what it *says*, many don't understand what it *means*. Many who choose to become pastors have absolutely no business in assuming such a lofty role. Pastors should typically know—and understand—more correct Biblical theology than a lay-person. But some of the most traditionally-uneducated Christians can out-Bible some of today's pastors. Homosexuality is clearly portrayed as an abomination in the Bible, however some major churches are ordaining gay pastors.

Even worse is the addition of transexual pastors. Not only do these pastors openly commit the sin of homosexuality, but they also seek to undermine the authority and wisdom of God in creating two genders and "assigning" one of these genders to that individual. A trans pastor, by his/her actions, is saying that God made a mistake in his/her creation. We follow the culture, rather than the Christ we claim to serve, and elevate such incompetent teachers. When we celebrate such overt sexual sins, Paul admonishes us, just as he admonished the church in 1 Corinthians 5:2. After his accusation, Paul instructs the church on the proper response to the situation. "When you are assembled in the name of our Lord Jesus and I am with you in spirit, and the power of our Lord Jesus is present, hand this man over to Satan, so that the sinful nature may be destroyed and his spirit saved on the day of the Lord" (1 Corinthians 5:4-5).

Excommunication is the appropriate answer—not elevating to a position of authority. We cannot accept the culture's imposition of changing our religious belief so long as those beliefs are Biblically sound. Paul continues his teaching with a statement you may remember from earlier in this book. Paul says, "But now I am writing you that you must not associate with anyone who calls himself a brother but is sexually immoral or greedy, an idolater or a slanderer, a drunkard or a swindler. With such a man do not even eat" (1 Corinthians 5:11). There's a list here and each is deserving of its place, but notice the sexually immoral people? Do not even eat with them! In other words, we shouldn't do anything that encourages people claiming to be followers of Christ to continue in their open, unrepentant sin. Yet we actually have pastors in all of these categories in America.

Some of these errant pastors even dare to go so far as to distort Scripture to support their claim that Jesus was homosexual or transexual—as if God, who has never made a single mistake, mistakenly assumed the wrong physical identity when he donned his mortal body. How do we fix it? Excommunication. It sounds harsh, but removing these people from the church, as Paul said, is to help them realize their sin, repent, and have their fellowship restored. Excommunication should be done as lovingly as possible, with the hopeful end result of the return of the wayward person—the return of the prodigal.

We remember the story of Sodom and Gomorrah, where the sin of homosexuality was so great and vile that God made fire rain from the sky to destroy both cities. We associate the sin of Sodom and Gomorrah so heavily with homosexual relations that the word sodomy was derived from Sodom. Homosexuality was definitely rampant in Sodom, as evidenced in Genesis 19, however God doesn't even put homosexuality first on the list of the city's sin. "Now this was the sin of your sister Sodom: She and her daughters were arrogant, overfed and unconcerned; they did not help the poor and needy. They were haughty and did detestable things before me. Therefore I did away with them as you have seen" (Ezekiel 16:49-50). Sodom committed some truly detestable acts, but that's the last item in God's list here. Of course, that's not to say their sins of homosexuality are unimportant. So why do Christians need to speak out about homosexuality so much when there are other "more important" sins? The short answer is that the ever-advancing homosexual agenda is a battle that is increasingly being forced upon Christianity, so we cannot remain silent. The slightly longer answer would add that we should (and do) speak out about the other sins as well when those battles arise.

With politicians all the way up to the level of Democratic Party presidential candidate eroding Christian beliefs, the complete distortion of true Christianity in all forms of entertainment, a large presence of severely lost so-called "Christians," and the knack of the majority of news outlets to push Christian values down, while lifting anti-Christian values up, America is becoming increasingly more hostile to Christianity. For example, Christians seeking only to protect our most vulnerable population, children, are viewed as unloving, hateful, control-seeking bigots. This of course extends to the topics of abortion, public school LGBTQ+ indoctrination, and perhaps in the very near future, the protection of children from "minor-attracted" adults—or as we should prefer to continue calling them, pedophiles.

Abortion advocates touted the "safe, legal, and rare" slogan until fairly recently. The "rare" in the slogan indicated a general understanding that abortion is not a good thing. In other words, it was a tacit admission that abortion was killing an innocent human. In recent years, the "safe, legal, and rare" slogan has fallen out of favor to make way for a more positive view on abortion. Now, abortion is often asserted as a moral good; sometimes viewed as a rite of passage, with some women even celebrating having had six or seven abortions. Bernie Sanders, another mainstream past presidential candidate, altered the phrase, saying "Abortion should be safe, legal and accessible to every person who chooses it."[5] I wonder if any of the murdered children chose abortion. A NY Times article says "Their language focuses on health care, bodily autonomy and, at times, even the idea of abortion as a positive force enabling women to control their lives and increase their economic security."[6] In our culture, when a Christian attempts to reasonably argue for the defense of innocent human life, he/she is attacked; usually verbally, but sometimes physically. Churches and Christian pregnancy help centers are vandalized, even being burned down in some cases. Can this be considered persecution in the United States?

Cling to the Truth

If you were being deceived, would you want to know? Undoubtedly you would. No one wants to be deceived. If this is the case, why would Christians, the group on earth that should be the most loving, let the world continue to be deceived? There are too many deceivers in the world to count. Jesus taught of the importance of truth in his famous statement "If you hold to my teaching, you are really my disciples. Then you will know the truth, and the truth will set you free" (John 8:31-32).

Truth is liberating and powerful. Truth does not care about your feelings. Truth is truth. If a statement is true, then that nugget of truth is true at all times and all places. There is no such thing as "my truth" or "your truth" or "his/her/their truth." Objective truth is not limited to what an individual knows or has experienced in the past. Truth does not rely on being perceived. If something is true, then it's true even if no one is aware of that

---

[5] Maggie Astor, "On Abortion Rights, 2020 Democrats Move Past 'Safe, Legal and Rare,'" *The New York Times*, November 25, 2019, https://www.nytimes.com/2019/11/25/us/politics/abortion-laws-2020-democrats.html.
[6] Astor, "Abortion Rights."

truth. Truth is constant; it doesn't change. We do not create truth, rather we observe it.

One enemy of truth is confirmation bias. As humans, we're all susceptible to this deception. In this case, we're deceiving ourselves by seeking out information that confirms our beliefs and ignoring information to the contrary. This bias affects both unbelievers and believers alike. Our God is the God of reason. Questioning Christianity is a good thing if the motives are right; those of seeking the truth, rather than simply confirming a contrary belief. Likewise, questioning beliefs in contradiction to Christian doctrine is a good thing. Following the truth will lead us to Jesus. In his own words, Jesus explained, "for this reason I was born, and for this I came into the world, to testify to the truth. Everyone on the side of truth listens to me" (John 18:37). So, when our children are honestly seeking the truth about Christ, we have nothing to fear! I say this logically, of course. Emotionally, I'm sure it *feels* differently when children come of age to be eternally accountable for their words and actions.

As American Christians, we're continually being conditioned to not only approve of homosexuality, but to support it. We fly flags and wear pins to support gay pride. We've learned that "love is love" and who are we to judge another person's love? We know that God loves all people and gay people are people, so God loves gay people. And we're told that these people are born gay, so it was God who made them that way. We can't really expect to be wiser than God, can we? If God created someone to be gay, then, we reason, surely he wanted them to be gay. Even though the Bible—God's Word—the Holy Scripture that Jesus himself held to be inerrant—expressly condemns homosexuality as an abomination. We've convinced ourselves that since homosexuality is performed by two consenting parties, there's no harm done. It's just love. It's something we can support. We'll wear a

As in the Days of Noah

pride pin. Soon, will we be wearing gender fluidity pins? Or right to "gender-affirming care" pins for transexual minors? Perhaps after that pin comes out, we'll move to wearing the "minor-attracted" persons pin to support pedophiles.

God doesn't support any of these causes, so why do we? Sin is sin. It's odd to support one type of sin and condemn another. As Christ's disciples, we should condemn all sin. Not that we ourselves are perfect by any means, but blatantly overt, unrepentant sin is a problem. Do you beat your wife? Let's get you a wife beater pin to show your support. Do you steal things? Let's get you a thief pin so other thieves know you stand with them. Do you cheat on your husband? It's the adultery pin for you! Wouldn't it be crazy to see Christians advertising their ongoing commission of these sins? What if they just advertised their support for people to continue committing these sins? "It's not for me, but who am I to judge?" Surely, you find this proposition as absurd as I do. Christians must not knowingly support sin, no matter what that sin is! The human that commits the sin is separate from that sin. Otherwise, Christ couldn't have taken *your* sin upon himself. All of these sinners can be saved, but they'll never feel any need to turn to God if they don't understand how their actions are in direct opposition to him.

Reason shouldn't just apply one way. If one side gets to assert their beliefs, while silencing the other side, then truth is not likely to be discovered. We've already mentioned the censorship and attacks Christians can face when speaking out against our culture's prized ideologies. Should this cause us to stop speaking the truth? When Peter and John were arrested for speaking the truth about Jesus, the authorities "commanded them not to speak or teach at all in the name of Jesus. But Peter and John replied, 'Judge for yourselves whether it is right in God's sight to obey you rather than God.'" (Acts 4:18-19). Is it right for us to obey the unbelievers of our day, rather than the God to whom we will all be held accountable?

Our words—what we choose to say and even when we choose to remain silent—have eternal weight (Matthew 12:36-37). "Anyone, then, who knows the good he ought to do and doesn't do it, sins" (James 4:17). If we know we should speak and don't, it is sin. This isn't to say that we must speak against every falsehood we encounter. When in a war, sometimes not fighting a battle is better for the overall goal. As a manager, when employees mess up, sometimes it's better to correct one, large issue today, rather than correcting the large issue *and* three or four smaller issues all at the same time. If I were to make every correction at one time, or even just make a correction every single time I see an error, my staff isn't going to like me much. They might lose respect for me or they may think that I'm just looking for a fight. Similarly, when we Christians find ourselves in discussion or debate with those that don't share our Biblical worldview, we may want to focus our attention on one or two major issues, rather than nitpicking everything that comes up in the conversation. If we took the latter approach, our conversation partner would likely be defensive and combative and not interested in giving any merit to the truth that we might proclaim to them.

When we find ourselves in these discussions, what should we say? There's a high probability that this type of conversation will be hard; awkward is the best scenario. In the worst scenario, it can bring physical, social, and/or financial danger. Paul advises, "Let your conversation be always full of grace, seasoned with salt, so that you may know how to answer everyone" (Colossians 4:6). We should seek to have our words be not only palatable, but delicious. As much as possible, view your conversation partner with the amount of grace God has afforded you in all your iniquities. You never know what might happen. You might end up learning something valuable from them!

Knowing that the workload can seem overly daunting at times, I regularly tell my employees that they're only responsible for doing the best job they're able. Once they're trained well enough to meet a baseline of productivity and quality, all I expect of them is an honest, good effort while they're at work. Anything beyond their capabilities given those parameters is not their concern. I think God views these situations the same. Argue in the defense of truth to your best ability and God will handle the rest according to his will. Jesus said, "When you are brought before synagogues, rulers and authorities, do not worry about how you will defend yourselves or what you will say, for the Holy Spirit will teach you at that time what you should say" (Luke 12:11-12).

Conclusion

We must choose a side. No choice is a choice. We either follow Christ or we don't. We either do what Christ says or we don't. We either believe Christ's words or we don't. Though it seems to be increasingly difficult nowadays, don't follow the masses on that wide highway that's leading them straight to death. Follow the narrow road that leads to life. This road might have potholes, sharp curves, and billboards telling us to take the next exit for the highway. In fact, it's almost guaranteed that we'll have difficulty on this road. Jesus said as much. See this mortal life as a training ground for eternity. Like Paul, "we also rejoice in our sufferings, because we know that suffering produces perseverance; perseverance, character; and character, hope" (Romans 5:3-4). But take solace in knowing our savior has overcome the world. We will bask in and share his glory for eternity.

We were made in the image of God, yet we constantly attempt to reshape God into our own image. This god we create is nothing but a mere idol. A dumb god, incapable of hearing, speech, or even movement. Such a god isn't worthy of worship. Why bother wasting time to create such a worthless being? Rather, we should worship and serve the true God of all creation. The one truly all-powerful being that created and sustains the universe; the one whose mere breath can form entire galaxies. Our God can route armies and part seas. He can see the end just as clearly as he sees the beginning. He sees, knows, and understands our deepest, darkest, most hidden parts—and he knew them all in intricate detail thousands of years ago. Our God created math. Our God created science. Our God created language. Geometry, algebra, and calculus; chemistry, biology, and physics; English, Spanish, verbs, participles, and prepositions—There is *nothing* possible without God. Stated another way, without God, there is nothing.

We have a responsibility to prepare ourselves to defend the truth of the gospel. This is implicit in the command to make disciples of all types of people. Jesus' Great Commission says we are to be making disciples, which includes "teaching them to obey everything I [Jesus] have commanded you" (Matthew 28:20). The only way to teach on a subject is to already know that subject matter. Jesus' command demands that we have knowledge of Scripture—not that we must be able to free-recall every Bible verse from memory, but that we know the nature of what it says. In other words, we must understand the "spirit of the law" when it comes to Scripture. This only comes through time and study. There are no easy ways around it. Read the Bible, spend time in prayer, and fast when necessary (see chapter 1 for more information on these disciplines of the faith).

If you know you have a major discussion coming in the near future, use the third faith discipline in conjunction with the other two. Fast and devote more time to prayer and study. Utilize those wise, Christ-honoring Christians in your life to gain their wisdom on the subject you expect to discuss. But don't rely on one-liners you might gain from them. Seek to understand for yourself both the issue and the reasons you believe the way you do.

While engaged in conversation or debate on hot-button cultural issues, there is no more time for preparation and study. When that time comes, we must say the good we know we should say, while understanding that not every battle must be waged at one time. Lean on the truth and don't deviate from it. It's okay to not know everything—no human does. In these moments, don't make something up to fill the void. Instead, just continue your honesty by saying you don't know the answer. Perhaps say something like, "That's a good point that I've never considered. I'll need to take some time to study it before I can draw any conclusions." You can even add, "Let's pick this conversation back up next time we see each other." If you use this, make sure you do what you say you're going to do! In this case, you must study the subject and/or continue the conversation at a later date.

Jesus warned us not to go along with the culture, rather we should follow him. At the end of the age, Jesus said people would continue on as they always have, not aware that judgment is coming. "Just as it was in the days of Noah, so also will it be in the days of the Son of Man. People were eating, drinking, marrying and being given in marriage up to the day Noah entered the ark. Then the flood came and destroyed them all" (Luke 17:26-27). People on the wide, easy highway to death will have no idea of the coming wrath. Jesus continues, "It was the same in the days of Lot. People were eating and drinking, buying and selling, planting and building. But the day Lot left Sodom, fire and sulfur rained down from heaven and destroyed them all" (Luke 17:28-29). The masses will continue living their lives as if nothing was coming; as if there are no consequences to disobeying God; as if God doesn't even exist.

Perhaps even worse than the oblivious masses are those who actively mock God and his revealed plans. Peter addresses this, saying "you must understand that in the last days scoffers will come, scoffing and following their own evil desires. They will say, 'Where is this "coming" he promised? Ever since our fathers died, everything goes on as it has since the beginning of creation'" (2 Peter 3:3-4). Scoff is a word we probably don't see very often in our daily lives. To put it simply, these people are mocking Jesus' promise of his return. Because they lack a belief in the coming judgment, they seek to please themselves, rather than seeking to please God. In terms we might hear today, they would say there's nothing better than to "follow your heart" or to "be true to yourself" or to "live your truth." And since the Lord, in his wisdom, has delayed his coming by two thousand years at this point, they are all the more emboldened to act as if he will never return; that there is no judgment.

As if he knew we would be struggling with this two thousand years later, Peter even addresses Jesus' delay, saying "But do not forget this one thing, dear friends: With the Lord a day is like a thousand years, and a thousand years are like a day. The Lord is not slow in keeping his promise, as some understand slowness. He is patient with you, not wanting anyone to perish, but everyone to come to repentance" (2 Peter 3:8-9). They don't realize that God isn't bound by time as we are. And his timing is perfect. The end will not come until the appointed time. When the last elect soul has been saved, then God's plan of redemption is complete and it will be time to render judgment on all those who are guilty—those whose sins have not been covered by the blood of Jesus.

Martin Luther King, Jr. had plenty of enemies in his time. Of course, he also had many allies. Now we dedicate a day to him every year to celebrate what he stood for. We celebrate Dr. King every year, all the while spitting on his grave. Dr. King would be appalled at the divisiveness we insist upon perpetuating in our culture. We allow false narratives to run rampant in our media and politics, destroying any semblance of unity we might foster across skin color divisions. We demand justice from the descendants of guilty parties as if they were the ones to commit the crime. Even worse, we teach young black children that the system is rigged against them and they will never be able to succeed because white people have the power. This is the most destructive thing you can beat down into a child's head. America is the freest country in the world. Black children can succeed if they are encouraged to do so. There are many successful black individuals. I imagine that most of these successful people had someone in their lives encouraging them to make something of themselves.

We could dive much deeper into each of these issues that are plaguing our culture. In fact, each one of these issues could fill the pages of its own book, but that's not the point of this volume. What's important to understand here is that the culture is against Christianity. Unfortunately, "the culture" also includes many of those Jesus would say are "lukewarm" Christians: self-professing Christians that have no idea what Jesus commands.

Will we have the strength to stand against the unbelieving culture? What if this leads to job loss? Will we have the resolve to stand against those who claim to follow Christ, yet clearly don't? What if this leads to social ostracization? Will we have the knowledge to refute those that know the words of the Bible, but twist the meaning to suit their own desires? What if this leads to physical attacks or imprisonment? Christianity is viewed more and more by our culture as toxic, unloving, and bigoted. We're seeing more and more cases of other countries passing laws to prevent Christians from speaking truth. Now—while we still have freedom in our country—is the time to prepare our hearts and minds; to take a stand for the truth; to decide whether Jesus will find us hot or cold.

We often like to think humanity has progressed and become more enlightened since ancient times, but humanity is all the same. As Solomon wisely stated, "What has been will be again, what has been done will be done again; there is nothing new under the sun" (Ecclesiastes 1:9). We chase our own modern idols today, just like the ancient Israelites chased theirs. The prophet Hosea delivered a message to corrupt ancient Israel that has chilling parallels to our own time. "The days of punishment are coming, the days of reckoning are at hand. Let Israel know this. Because your sins are so many and your hostility so great, the prophet is considered a fool, the inspired man a maniac" (Hosea 9:7). This sounds a lot like our culture. Those who would seek to know and follow Christ's commands are seen as fools. True Christians are ridiculed for their beliefs at every turn. Christianity is a prime target for today's culture. Will you hold up under the pressure? Do you even know enough about what you believe to understand why what the culture admires is evil? There is no fence to sit on. Choose your side, then solidify your knowledge. Stand on the truth, because there is no firmer ground.

Epilogue

We are in the end times! In fact, we've been in the end times for two thousand years. So, when is the end? I don't know. But what I, like the Apostle Paul, can say with absolute certainty, is we are "nearer now than when we first believed" (Romans 13:11). Honestly, I can't imagine that we're relatively far from the end of the age. Regardless, time continues moving forward. We are closer than we were yesterday. Through the prophet Daniel, we learn that at the conclusion of the end times, "Many will be purified, made spotless and refined, but the wicked will continue to be wicked. None of the wicked will understand, but those who are wise will understand" (Daniel 12:10). Is it possible for this to be a more accurate description of the culture in which we live?

The wicked don't understand Christianity. In fact, Christian messaging—truth, in other words—is often censored as misinformation or disinformation. Those messages that aren't censored are attacked as racist, bigoted, misogynistic, hateful, and control-seeking. With the massive, concerted effort to censor and destroy true Christian dialogue, can we really doubt that there are spiritual forces at play? "For our struggle is not against flesh and blood, but against the rulers, against the authorities, against the powers of this dark world and against the spiritual forces of evil in the heavenly realms" (Ephesians 6:12). We all serve one of two masters, whether we realize it or not. Either we serve God or we serve the devil. Those who serve the devil have been deceived. Their evil ideologies undoubtedly need to be defeated by sound logic. But more than anything, these individuals need prayer. Perhaps through sound logic and God's providence, we might gain a powerful ally in this spiritual battle. Far more importantly, we might gain a brother or sister whose friendship we can enjoy for eternity. Even the Apostle Paul persecuted Christians to the point of death before his conversion.

Choose your relationships carefully. No man is an island. What we allow to feed our minds will ultimately begin to come out of us. "Blessed is the man who does not walk in the counsel of the wicked or stand in the way of sinners or sit in the seat of mockers. But his delight is in the law of the Lord, and on his law he meditates day and night" (Psalm 1:1-2). Distance yourself from self-proclaimed Christians that demonstrate their lack of salvation through constant, blatant, unrepentant sin. This also extends to those teaching a false gospel message. Those we might wish to reach with the true gospel will judge us by our associations. Perhaps even worse, a genuine seeker might believe our association with a false teacher gives credit to that teaching. None of this is to say we should avoid unbelievers—those that don't claim to be Christians (1 Corinthians 5:10). Our divinely-ordered commission requires dealing with unbelievers.

When you're on an airplane, part of the routine safety information they go over is in the event the oxygen masks deploy, you need to put your own mask on before helping anyone else. Our Christian walk is largely the same in this regard. As Paul says, "Put on the full armor of God so that you can take your stand against the devil's schemes" (Ephesians 6:11). Above all, we must focus on our own Christian walk. Set up for yourself a firm Christian foundation. "Be joyful always; pray continually; give

Epilogue

thanks in all circumstances, for this is God's will for you in Christ Jesus" (1 Thessalonians 5:16-18). Read the Bible regularly—every day is best. No one can don your armor for you; you must put forth your own effort to do so.

I can think of no better way to end this book than with some words from the wisest man to have lived. Solomon's thesis for life gives instruction, warning, and encouragement. "Now all has been heard; here is the conclusion of the matter: Fear God and keep his commandments, for this is the whole duty of man. For God will bring every deed into judgement, including every hidden thing, whether it is good or evil" (Ecclesiastes 12:13-14).

Acknowledgements

First and foremost, thank you, God, for aligning my life in the exact manner necessary to bring me to this precise point. Thank you for the good and the bad, the sweet and the mad, the happy and the sad, the discontent and the glad. Thank you for that cheesy rhyming sentence too.

To everyone who played a role in the creation of this book, knowingly or unknowingly, thank you. Writing an actual book is something I've wanted to do for a very long time, but never thought it was really a possibility. Every interaction in my life has led to this outcome. If you've played any role in my life, this book was your doing as well.

Thank you, Benjamin Hardy, for writing *Willpower Doesn't Work*. I certainly didn't follow your advice to a T, but your book provided the spark.

Thank you, Heather, for believing in my writing abilities despite only having received work-related emails from me. Your encouragement to follow my nearly-forsaken dream provided the tinder.

Thank you to all the ministries that have impacted me and helped me to grow in the knowledge of Scripture. Perhaps particular thanks are due to Dr. Frank Turek and his work with Cross Examined. Your wisdom provided the fuel.

And last, but certainly not least, thank you to my wife, Nina. Thank you for your unwavering support of me, regardless of whatever crazy scheme I decide to chase. Thank you for cleaning up my messes. Thank you for unselfishly putting me first on so many occasions. Your atmosphere of love and support provided the oxygen.

More importantly, Nina, thank you for providing a safe, loving home for my children. Thank you for the deep, motherly bond you've formed with my sons. And thank you for your dedication to turning them into good adult humans.

Thank you, Samuel and Lucas, for being my sons. I know you're too young to read this right now, but maybe one day you'll see it. I enjoy being a father far more than I ever thought I would. Thank you for giving me the opportunity.

Bibliography

Allers, Roger and Rob Minkoff. *The Lion King*. United States: Walt Disney Pictures, 1994.

Alzheimer's San Diego. "Facts & Stats." Accessed July 19, 2023, https://www.alzsd.org/resources/facts-stats/.

American Auto Insurance. "What Color Car Gets Pulled Over the Most?" July 23, 2020. https://www.americanautoinsurance.com/blog/what-color-car-gets-pulled-over-the-most/.

Astor, Maggie. "On Abortion Rights, 2020 Democrats Move Past 'Safe, Legal and Rare.'" *The New York Times*, November 25, 2019. https://www.nytimes.com/2019/11/25/us/politics/abortion-laws-2020-democrats.html.

Avildsen, John G. *The Karate Kid*. United States: Columbia Pictures, 1984.

Barna, George. *American Worldview Inventory 2021-2022*. Arizona: Arizona Christian University Press, 2022.

Blackley, Julie. "Most Popular Car Colors." Accessed August 4, 2023. https://www.iseecars.com/most-popular-car-colors-study.

Boutselis, Pamme. "SNHU Affirms Alignment with National Campaign to #SeeAll." September 23, 2019. https://www.snhu.edu/about-us/newsroom/community/snhu-affirms-alignment-to-seeall.

Casting Crowns, "One Step Away." Track 3 on *The Very Next Thing*. Provident Distribution, 2016, compact disc.

Clark, Bob. *A Christmas Story*. United States: Metro-Goldwyn-Mayer, 1983.

Cross Examined. "How to STOP to interpret the Bible." January 23, 2020. YouTube video, 04:06. https://youtu.be/WhZsSQLf7wc.

Daniels, Greg, writer and director. *The Office*. Season 4, episode 1, "Fun Run." Aired September 27, 2007. https://www.peacocktv.com/watch/playback/vod/GMO_000 00000007428_01/41f1443a-a633-3618-a85f-cbcfca438e31?paused=true.

Delbridge, Emily. "What Is the Most Popular Car Color?" April 26, 2020. https://www.liveabout.com/most-popular-car-colors-4160630.

Dictionary.com. s.v. "Hermeneutics." Accessed July 21, 2023. https://www.dictionary.com/.

Federal Reserve Bank of New York. "Household Debt and Credit Report (Q1 2023)." Accessed July 20, 2023. https://www.newyorkfed.org/microeconomics/hhdc.

Francois, Paul and Enrique Garcia. "Studying Liars Part I." December 1, 2011. https://www.tdcorg.com/article/studying-liars-part-i/.

Friel, Todd. "Sin Wants You." *Wretched Radio*, June 2, 2023. Podcast, 51:52. https://wretched.org.radio/.

Jennings, Garth. *The Hitchhiker's Guide to the Galaxy*. United States: Touchstone Pictures, 2005.

King, Martin Luther, Jr. "I Have a Dream." (speech, March on Washington for Jobs and Freedom, Lincoln Memorial, Washington DC, August 28, 1963). https://www.npr.org/2010/01/18/122701268/i-have-a-dream-speech-in-its-entirety.

Bibliography

Kochhar, Rakesh. "How Americans compare with the global middle class." July 9, 2015. https://www.pewresearch.org/fact-tank/2015/07/09/how-americans-compare-with-the-global-middle-class/.

Lewis, C. S. *God in the Dock*, edited by Walter Hooper. Michigan: Wm. B. Eerdmans Publishing Co., 2014.

McKay, Adam. *Talladega nights: The Ballad of Ricky Bobby*. United States: Columbia Pictures, 2006.

Metaxas, Eric. *Letter to the American Church*. Washington, D.C.: Salem Books, 2022.

National Football League. "NFL offseason workout program dates announced for all 32 teams ahead of 2022 NFL season." April 1, 2022. www.nfl.com/_amp/nfl-offseason-workout-program-dates-announced-ahead-of-2022-season-for-all-32-te.

Norman, Kayda. "Average Car Insurance Rates by Age and Gender." April 22, 2022. https://www.nerdwallet.com/article/insurance/car-insurance-rates-age-gender.

Raimi, Sam. *Spider-Man*. United States: Columbia Pictures, 2002.

Roosevelt, Eleanor. *You Learn by Living*. New York: HarperCollins Publishers, 1960.

Staff. "How Many Miracles Are There In The Bible?" February 28, 2019. https://www.spiritoflifeag.com/how-many-miracles-are-there-in-the-bible/.

Suciu, Peter. "Americans Spent On Average More Than 1,300 Hours On Social Media Last Year." June 24, 2021. https://www.forbes.com/sites/petersuciu/2021/06/24/americans-spent-more-than-1300-hours-on-social-media/?sh=71d3d15c2547.

Tamás, Viktória, Ferenc Kocsor, Petra Gyuris, Noémi Kovács, Endre Czeiter, and András Büki, "The Young Male Syndrome—An Analysis of Sex, Age, Risk Taking and Mortality in Patients With Severe Traumatic Brain Injuries." Front. Neurol. 10 (2019). https://doi.org/10.3389%2Ffneur.2019.2019.00366.

The Holy Word Church of God. "How Many Words In The Bible." Accessed July 19, 2023. https://holyword.church/miscellaneous-resources/how-many-words-in-the-bible/.

Thiessen, Marc. "Hillary Clinton's war on faith." *New York Post*, October 15, 2016. http://nypost.com/2016/10/15/hillary-clintons-war-on-faith/.

Tomlin, Chris, "Whom Shall I Fear." Track 3 on *Burning Lights*. sixstepsrecords, Sparrow Records, 2013, compact disc.

Turek, Frank. "15 Mistakes We Make Judging God's Morality – Part 1." *I Don't Have Enough Faith to Be An Atheist*, October 7, 2022. Podcast, 48:15. https://crossexamined.org/podcasts/.

Turek, Frank. "The Universe Had a Beginning." December 29, 2011. https://crossexamined.org/the-universe-had-a-beginning/.

Tyson, Neil DeGrasse. *Astrophysics for People in a Hurry*. New York: W. W. Norton & Company, Inc, 2017.

Wallace, J. Warner. *Cold-Case Christianity*. Colorado: David C Cook, 2013.

whatever. "He Made Her RAGE QUIT?! (STORMS OUT) | Dating Talk #33." November 3, 2022. YouTube video, 03:41:47. https://www.youtube.com/watch?v=cVsgbz0pFIY.

Wretched. "Four steps of interpreting Scripture." December 24, 2018. YouTube video, 05:23. https://youtu.be/-Wvt8LTAdaw.

Scripture Index

Genesis
1:1 .... 63, 174
3 175
4 134
18 71
18:20-32 18
18:25 19
18:27 18
18:30 18
18:31 18
18:32 18
19 191
37-50 169
50:20 171

Exodus
Book of 20
1 135
1:15-21 135
3:14 66
4:10-13 38
4:11 44
20:17 KJV 158
30:20-21 11

Leviticus
20:10 87

Deuteronomy
7:4 102
17:17 102
23:14 11

32:35 134

Joshua
2-6 135

1 Samuel
Book of 147
13:14 171
21:10-15 135

2 Samuel
Book of 147
11:27 172

1 Kings
11:3 102

2 Kings
2:9-14 97
15-17 97

1 Chronicles
29:11 81

2 Chronicles
9:13-28 160

Job
Book of 68
1:8 126
38:2-3 68
38:4-5 68

38-41 68
42:3 68
42:5-6 69

Psalms
Book of 70
1:1-2 204
51 172
51:7 136
88 .... 50, 70-71
88:1 71
88:18 70
90:2 66
101:6-7 114
119:105 9
139:1-6 80
147:4 66

Proverbs
Book of 133, 173
5:3-6 117
5:6 117
12:9 159
12:26 101
13:20 114
14:12 116
15:3 66
17:22 113
19:18 53
20:27 117
21:23 133
22:6 109

Scripture Index

22:24-25 ... 112	**Micah**	25:30 ... 41
25:21-22 ... 133-134	6:8 ... 111	25:33 ... 95
27:5 ... 126		28:19 . 105, 125, 137
27:17 ... 111	**Habakkuk**	28:20 ... 198
29:20 ... 138	Book of ... 112	
		Mark
Ecclesiastes	**Matthew**	12:29-30 ... 123
Book of ... 173	3:8 ... 186	12:31 ... 123
1:9 ... 202	3:9 ... 186	
2:10-11 ... 159-160	3:12 ... 95	**Luke**
12:13-14 ... 205	5:28 ... 116	9:57-62 ... 128
	5:37 ... 136	9:62 ... 128
Song of Songs	5:39 ... 133	12:11-12 ... 197
Book of ... 173	6:7-8 ... 23	12:47-48 43-44, 117
	6:9 ... 25	12:51 ... 95
Isaiah	6:9-13 KJV ... 24	17:26-27 ... 199
1:18 ... 111	6:10 ... 25	17:28-29 ... 199-200
46:10 ... 76	6:11 ... 25	18:1-8 ... 30
	6:12 ... 25	18:5 ... 30
Ezekiel	6:13 ... 25	18:6-8 ... 30-31
3:18-19 ... 119	6:20 ... 47	19:12-27 ... 40
16:49-50 ... 191	6:24 ... 93	19:13 ... 40
	7:1 ... 121	19:23 ... 41
Daniel	7:3 ... 121	19:27 ... 41
Book of ... 177	7:5 ... 121-122	
3:17-18 ... 177	7:6 ... 122	**John**
10:3 ... 30	7:13-14 ... 99, 187	1:1-3 ... 85, 96
12:2 ... 176	7:21-23 ... 2, 91	2:15 ... 95
12:9 ... 81	7:22-23 ... 29	5:24 ... 90
12:10 ... 203	10:28 ... 1	8:2-11 ... 86
	10:31 ... 33	8:7 ... 87
Hosea	12:35 ... 47	8:11 ... 55, 87
9:7 ... 202	12:36 ... 187	8:31-32 ... 193
	12:36-37 ... 196	8:44 ... 136
Amos	13:44-46 ... 27	8:58 ... 67
5:12 ... 117	13:47-50 ... 28	10:26-30 ... 89
	21:12 ... 121	10:28 ... 127
Jonah	23 ... 121	10:28-29 ... 88
Book of ... 38	23:33 ... 121	11:41-42 ... 70
1:17 ... 38	24:12 ... 2	12:30 ... 70
	25:14-30 ... 40, 118	

14:6 187	25:27 41	4:25 136
14:15 123	12:2 2	4:29 138
16:32 180	12:3 127	5:4 134
16:33 .... 99, 180	12:6-8 38	6:11 204
18:37 194	13:11 203	6:12 .... 2, 31, 203
19:30 33	15:24 173	6:19-20 138
21:19 158		6:20 103
21:22 158	**1 Corinthians**	
21:25 21	1:25 67	**Philippians**
	3:6 2	1:9-11 13-14
Acts	5:1-2 124	3:1 13
4:18-19 195	5:2 190	4:11-13 47
5:29 76	5:4-5 190	4:13 NKJV 77
5:39 77	5:5 124	
13:22 171	5:10 .... 105, 204	**Colossians**
17:10-12 141	5:11 ... 105, 190-191	1:15-17 75
	6:9-11 55	4:6 196
Romans	6:12-20 129	
1:13 174	9:24 43	**1 Thessalonians**
1:20 62	9:24-27 185	5:16-18 204-205
2:15 37	10:21 188	5:25 149
3:10 .... 35, 116	11:32 54	
3:10-18 116	15:19 90	**1 Timothy**
3:23 .... 35, 124	15:33 112	1:15 55
5:3-4 197	15:53-54 92	3:14-15 173
5:8 58		
5:20 .... 51, 86	**2 Corinthians**	**2 Timothy**
6:2 86	5:10 43	2:3-4 185
6:3-14 87	6:14 113	2:5 185
6:12 87	7:1 113	3:5 122
6:16 93	9:6 47	4:6-8 185
6:18 94	11:21-12:10 58	4:7-8 98-99
6:21 94	13:5 29	
6:22 94		**Hebrews**
6:23 94	**Galatians**	6:6 98
7:15-25 86	5:17 86	6:7-8 46
7:19 58	5:22-23 17, 113-114	6:18 78
8:26-27 23		9:14 171
8:28 .... 112, 167, 175	**Ephesians**	10:19-22 16
8:38-39 88-89	1:11 57	11 135
9:20-21 56	1:13 46	11:31 135
9:22 56	1:14 46	13:8 77

Scripture Index

James
Book of 36
1:5 17
1:6-8 .... 17, 31
1:12 42
1:19 134
1:22 15
2:18 36
2:19 37
2:26 37
3:3 132
3:4-5 132
3:5-6 132
3:8 132
4:2 17
4:3 17
4:17 196
5:12 136

5:16 17

1 Peter
1:13-16 125
2:11-12 125
2:12 103
3:15 .... 45, 90
4:2-3 115
4:3 55
5:8 126

2 Peter
1:2 15
3:3-4 200
3:8-9 200
3:10 98
3:16 149-150
3:18 13

1 John
1:8 116
1:10 116
2:19 89

2 John
7 105
10-11 105

Revelation
1:5-6 16
1:8 81
3:15-16 185
3:20 188
5:5 .... 95, 121
12:12 2
19:11-16 96

Printed in the USA
CPSIA information can be obtained
at www.ICGtesting.com
LVHW021601181123
764201LV00013B/104

9 798989 119608